Veronica Brady:
A Living Legacy

A Forum for a Theology in the World
Volume 4, Issue 1&2, 2017

A Forum for a Theology in the World is an academic refereed journal aimed at engaging with issues in the contemporary world, a world which is pluralist and eucumenical in nature. The journal reflects this pluralism and ecumenism. Each edition is theme specific and has its own editor responsible for the production. The journal aims to elicit and encourage dialogue on topics and issues in contemporary society and within a variety of religious traditions. The Editor in Chief welcomes submissions of manuscripts, collections of articles, for review from individuals or institutions, which may be from seminars or conferences or written specifically for the journal. An internal peer review is expected before submitting the manuscript. It is the expectation of the publisher that, once a manuscript has been accepted for publication, it will be submitted according to the house style to be found at the back of this volume. All submissions to the Editor in Chief are to be sent to: hdregan@atf.org.au.

Each edition is available as a journal subscription, or as a book in print, pdf or epub, through the ATF Press web site — www.atfpress.com. Journal subscriptions are also available through EBSCO and other library suppliers.

Editor in Chief
Hilary Regan, ATF Press

A Forum for a Theology in the World is published by ATF Theology and imprint of
ATF (Australia) Ltd (ABN 90 116 359 963) and
is published twice or three times a year.
ISSN 1329-6264

Soft cover	978-1-925643-75-6
Hardback	978-1-925643-76-3
epub	978-1-925643-77-0
pdf	978-1-925643-78-7

ATF Press
PO Box 504
Hindmarsh SA 5007
Australia
www.atfpress.com

Subscription Rates 2017

Print	On-Line	Print and On-line
Aust $65 Individuals	Aus $55 individuals	Aus $75 individuals
Aus $90 Institutions	Aus $80 individuals	Aus $100 instiutions

Veronica Brady:
A Living Legacy

ATF Theology
Adelaide
2017

Table of Contents

Preface

This publication had its origins in a Symposium '*Veronica Brady: A Living Legacy*', held at the University of Western Australia, 5 February, 2016. The Symposium was organised by Tony Hughes-d'Aeth and *The Westerly Centre* at the University of Western Australia and, as a result of the strong sense of the value of Brady's life and work that arose from the day's talks, it was thought that a collection of some of the papers would be of value to the many who are interested in Brady but were unable to attend. All of the papers included here, with the exception of the Introduction and the essays by Toby Davidson, Kieran Dolin and Gail Jones, were delivered at the Symposium

Jones has kindly permitted the reprinting of her '*Dark Places*: The Movement of the Image (Thoughts on the work of Veronica Brady)' and we thank *Coolabah* for permission to reprint this essay here. Thanks also go to Dylan Hyde for help with biographical material. Finally we record our deep appreciation, to Hilary Regan of ATF Press for his editorial advice and wholehearted support of this publication.

Kieran Dolin, Tony Hughes-d'Aeth and Dominic Hyde (Editors)

Introduction

Dominic Hyde, Leigh Dale and Kieran Dolin

Veronica Brady was born on January 5 1929 and christened 'Patricia Brady', later taking the name 'Veronica' when she joined the Institute for the Blessed Virgin Mary (IBVM)—the Sisters of Loreto. She was born of Irish-Australian Catholic parents in Melbourne, Australia, but by the time she started school the family had moved to country Victoria. Already able to read and write, she entered third grade under 'The Sisters Without Mercy', as her father called them. After several years the family returned to Melbourne, and the extended family that coalesced in the Hawthorn and Caulfield area, and Brady attended Loreto Mandeville.

Finishing school at fifteen, she went on to study History and English at Melbourne University. Her love of language was not surprising. Her father, Ted Brady, was undoubtedly a strong influence. He was known to frequently recite Australian poetry to his guests at home. Paterson's 'The Man From Ironbark' was a favourite and, with a few drinks under his belt, he would mount the table and screech 'murder, bloody murder, yelled the man from Ironbark!' to the delight of his children. (Whether his guests were equally delighted is not known.) Fond of puns, Ted seemed to revel in the delights of language. 'Have you ever seen a-bun-dance?', he would joke with his young daughter, pointing to a well-provisioned table and wiggling a bun. And books had been prominent from a very young age, with *Winnie the Pooh* and *The Magic Pudding* remaining favourites until Brady's final days. Another family favourite was Don Marquis' *Archy and Mehitabel*—the tales of Archy the cockroach and Mehitabel the alley cat. Mehitabel's declaration 'there's a dance in the old dame yet' was a favourite quote of Brady's in later life, as was Mehitabel's refrain 'toujours gai toujours gai'.

Traces of her father can also be discerned in Brady's life-long political activism. Her father—a committed pacifist of whom it was said that 'no amount of prosperity could have weaned him from his allegiance to the party of the working man'—would, no doubt, have been proud of the moniker sometimes used to describe Brady: 'the Red Nun'. Not long after she was born, in a magazine issued by the company where Ted worked, it was reported that:

> In private life, Mr Brady is widely known and in constant demand as a speaker. He is a keen student of politics and therein his political speeches differ from those of the average politician. As an after-dinner speaker he is positively brilliant.

Somewhat presciently adding:

> Mr Brady is well known in racing circles and is an ardent follower of the turf. As a globe trotter he is, according to Mr Marcus Burke (his nephew), the ideal companion. Despite these varied activities we have it on the highest authority that Mr Brady's predominating interest in life is the youthful Miss Brady, who *despite her comparatively recent arrival in this world is already giving evidence of an inheritance of her father's wit*.[1]

Brady's much-loved mother Alice was frequently talked about with a softness bordering on melancholy, and always with enormous love. She died before the age of fifty from heart problems—a tragic loss to the family that cast a sad shadow. Brady was in her first year of university at the time.

A few months after graduating in late 1949 she entered the convent. And in the first year of her novitiate she began to follow the teaching tradition of the Loreto Sisters, starting at Loreto Mandeville. She later moved on to teach at Loreto institutions at Ballarat and Kirribilli, and took her final vows in 1957. It was at Kirribilli that she first stumbled across Patrick White's *The Tree of Man*. She was immediately enthralled. And when in 1966, somewhat unusually for the times, she was chosen by the Order to undertake postgraduate studies abroad, it was Patrick White that she would focus on.

1.　*TM Bourke Co. Magazine*, unpublished (1929), 5. Italics added.

Brady studied initially for a Masters at the University of Chicago, encountering Paul Tillich and Mircea Eliade, who would become formative influences on her work. 'Theology was intellectually respectable there', Brady later wrote in *Caught in the Draught*.[2] Here she found herself in the heartland of the American civil rights movement—a factor in her later involvement in campaigns for Aboriginal justice—and also witnessed the beginnings of the Vietnam anti-war movement. Her political 'education' continued when she moved to the University of Toronto, where she encountered numerous American students dodging the draft down south. Among the elective courses she took was one on Blake with the famous Canadian theorist, Northrop Frye. In 1969 she completed her thesis on Patrick White—one of the first PhDs on Australian literature.

On her return to Australia more teaching ensued, including lecturing trainee teachers at Melbourne's Christ College and tutoring at St Mary's College, but she hankered for more intellectually stimulating work in a university. The head of the Loreto order gave permission, and she applied for a position as Senior Tutor in English at the University of Western Australia (UWA). This, her first application, was successful and in 1972 she headed west with the added joy of being reunited with her sister Marie, now living in Perth with nine children and married to a solid-state chemist, Dr Bruce Hyde, also then working at UWA.

It is worth bearing in mind how singular her position was. She was a woman in a decidedly man's world, and a nun to boot—the only nun in Australia then with a tenured university post. Since the church reforms of Vatican II, she had abandoned the sombre black and white habit of nuns before her but a nun she remained (living in the Loreto community in Nedlands, Perth, until she finally moved into independent accommodation later in her life). And she was a specialist in Australian Literature in a department that taught no Australian literature.

That situation was soon to change with accomplices like Bruce Bennett, Dorothy Hewett, Peter Cowan, Fay Zwicky, and John Beston, and within a few years Australian Literature became a feature of the English Department's curriculum and, increasingly, a focus of Brady's research.

---

2. Veronica Brady, *Caught in the Draught* (Sydney: Angus and Robertson, 1994), 7.

Patrick White was central to the teaching and research of Australian Literature as it began to emerge as a subject in Australian universities, especially after he was awarded the Nobel Prize for Literature in 1973. At a conference devoted to his work held at Flinders University in Adelaide in 1978, Brady spoke on White's dialogue with Simone Weil. Prompted in part by her argument that White's writing had deeper affiliations with the tradition of 'Wisdom literature' than with the genre of the novel, and in part by the multiplicity of critical methodologies on display, the volume of papers published from the conference included an appendix containing short theoretical reflections by John Colmer and Brady. Colmer defended a formalist and ethical approach centred on the text, while Brady argued for an openness to the philosophical and symbolic dimensions of White's language and structures. This early statement usefully captures Brady's critical *credo*:

> No work has its meaning alone. On the contrary, its implications are affected not only by patterns of sensibility and value but also by the sense of possibility at work within the culture to which the reader belongs.[3]

Here, Brady's deep commitment to literature as enabling a critical reflection on the society in which it was produced is evident. With her familiarity with modern philosophy and theology, as well as her North American postgraduate work, Brady was an informed and independent participant in the theoretical debates that swept through literary studies in the 1980s. She adhered to no 'school' of criticism, and saw theories as tools that could offer a deeper understanding of texts and culture.

Brady was perhaps uniquely placed to engage critically with the range and depth of White's *oeuvre*. He is the subject of the only chapter in *A Crucible of Prophets: Australians and the Question of God* that was devoted to a single author. She demonstrates a sympathetic understanding of the writer's ambitious project of reconfiguring Australian sensibilities, not least through devastating portrayals of the mundane, the rational, the conventional and the literal. With her

---

3. Veronica Brady, 'Appendix 2', *Patrick White: A Critical Symposium*, edited by Ron Shepherd and Kirpal Singh (Adelaide: Centre for Research in the New Literatures in English, 1978), 140.

interests in the apocalyptic Christianity of writers like William Blake, and her knowledge of competing western religious traditions and the philosophical writers who engaged with them, Brady was well placed to offer an engagement with White's complex and sometimes contradictory portrayals of spiritual experience. That White valued her critical commentary is evidenced by his dedicating *Memoirs of Many in One* to 'the Red Nun.' In one of her best essays, 'A Properly Appointed Humanism: Australian Culture and the Aborigines in Patrick White's *A Fringe of Leaves*', she draws on the anthropologist Levi-Strauss to contrast Aboriginal culture's social ethics and attitude to nature with those of white society. In Brady's critical practice, spiritual insights had social and political consequences.

Brady reflected on the mental structures of settler colonialism, and meaningful forms of engagement with and reparation for Indigenous Australians, principally in *Can These Bones Live?*—first delivered as the New College Lectures at the University of New South Wales in 1988—and in many essays, such as those collected in *Caught in the Draught*. In these works, postcolonial writers such as Edward Said and Frantz Fanon supplement the European hermeneutic thinkers she had always been drawn to, Gadamer and Ricoeur, and Aboriginal writers such as Bill Neidjie provide alternative perspectives on inhabiting Australia to the fraught literary place-making of White, Randolph Stow and Judith Wright.

Brady presented her challenging interpretations of Australian literature and society in a great variety of general and professional publications outside the university and literary sectors. She also was a courageous public speaker, and often spoke at rallies, public meetings, seminars and small group events. Despite her diminutive stature, she spoke with energy and conviction, radiating intellectual and moral force. During her career at UWA she became the most-widely known member of its English Department, a public intellectual with the capacity to address a broad audience on subjects related to literature, politics and spirituality. As Leigh Dale recalls, she was sought after as a speaker (like her father before her) and an interviewee, even appearing on the ABC comedy program *Good News Week* where she played up to the host's shock at her violation of stereotypes about older women and nuns.

Upon her retirement in 1994, Brady began a number of new projects, including a major biography of the poet Judith Wright, *South of My Days*. In it she demonstrated that the environmental and political activism of Wright's later career was closely related to the concerns of her poetry. In the second half of the 1990s, Brady became a trustee of Australian Theological Forum's Literary Trust, and in 1999 she became co-editor with Hilary Regan of its 'Faith in the Public Forum' series. In 2008 ATF Press published one of Brady's last books, the essay collection, *The God-Shaped Hole: Responding to the Good News in Australia*.

As a teacher, Brady was sometimes intimidating but always sympathetic to those students who made the effort to prepare for her classes. She regarded creative writers as special beings who should be supported where possible and sought to instill this view in others. (Knowing some students aspired to book reviewing, she once remarked in a tutorial that it was important to be large-hearted, unless a writer used demeaning stereotypes in which case being critical was a 'duty'.) She was generous with her time and her personal library—her kindness was often discreet, whilst her dissent from conventions she thought oppressive or unjust was public.

As a colleague, Brady was encouraging, and deeply involved in the collective life of the department. She was an attentive listener and ready arguer in research seminars, often inviting the speaker to probe further in their inquiries, and reflect on the social significance of their arguments, in effect, versions of the 'so what?' question. She kept up with new theories, recognizing the power of new concepts, but was skeptical about jargon. At a seminar for secondary English teachers designed to introduce the keyword of 'representation,' she responded to participants' difficulties with the new term by suggesting they just use the word 'image' instead. While relating the new learning to their existing knowledge, this advice did rather scupper the new vocabulary!

Her efforts were not confined to academic and indigenous issues, however. She became increasingly outspoken on religious issues as well. Just as her religious views led very directly, as she saw it, to the need to call out social injustice—and she did, in print, radio and television interviews, street marches and public rallies—they also led her to very publicly call for what she saw as essential reforms in the

Catholic church—including more progressive attitudes to abortion, contraception, homosexuality and the ordination of women.

Active participation in public life, alongside the reflective life of an academic and nun, with the material means for existence taken care of with the minimum of effort and fuss, hers was a life of ideas and associated action.

Also an avid cyclist, Brady was regularly seen pedaling to work on her bike, 'Xavier', persisting well into her 70s, enjoying what Gail Jones has described as her 'Franciscan rejoicing in simple accelera-tion'. This was part of a larger commitment to humility and solidarity with the poor that shaped her attitude to material things, and also speaks to her late life interest in the environment that included a Rockefeller Fellowship to the University of Oregon at Eugene.

Throughout her adult life and into old age, Veronica Brady dem-onstrated a capacity for renewal, taking on new projects, engaging with new thinkers and books, and inspiring those younger scholars and friends with her intellectual passion. She was a *generative* person in the sense used by Erikson in his stages of identity. Though regu-larly quoting Judith Wright's dictum that 'old age ain't for sissies', she embodied intellectual creativity. She died on 20 August 2015 in West-ern Australia at the age of 86.[4]

---

4. A fuller account of Brady's life can be found in Kath Jordan's biography, *Larrikin Angel*, published by Roundhouse Press in 2009.

Recollections and Encounters

Veronica's Earl Grey and Brady's *The Mystics*

Toby Davidson

I first heard of Veronica Brady (with and without the 'Sister') when I was an undergraduate at the University of Western Australia from the mid-1990s. Tutors and friends who shared my metaphysical interests would independently ask 'Do you know Veronica Brady?' Most showed genuine pity when I was forced to admit I did not even know *of* her, and a few sought to fill me in with arias about her nous, her advice, her wit and her pluck. It wasn't that this legendary figure was 'cool' (not like The Prodigy or Oasis), but she was *real*, and truth-tellers, those who spoke truth to power, as Edward Said famously put it[1], were in short supply for a young man despairing at John Howard's wilful blindness to history, to compassion, to education—qualities for which he is still loudly celebrated. I can only hope Veronica Brady is celebrated just as loudly, and for longer, because what she stood for, and equally stood up for, represents everything that privileged, paranoid Australian nationalism denies but can never defeat.

In 2005 I began my PhD on Christian mysticism in Australian poetry at Deakin University, and 'Do you know Veronica Brady?' quickly became 'You *have* to talk to Veronica Brady'. It wasn't a suggestion. On a trip back to Perth, I looked up her phone number (Brady, V, Nedlands) and made the call, anxiously aware that I knew little of her work beyond *South of My Days,*[2] her masterful biography of Judith Wright. She answered, and I fumbled through a quick explanation: *Poetry . . . mysticism . . . I was told to call you.* She seemed

---

1. Edward, Said, *Representations of the Intellectual: The 1993 Reith Lectures* (London: Vintage, 1994).
2. Veronica Brady, *South of My Days: A Biography of Judith Wright* (Pymble. Angus & Robertson, 1998).

unsurprised; clearly I was not the first proto-scholar sent her way. Her immediate warmth and sincerity put me at ease. When we met at her small flat off Stirling Highway, I realised I had seen an image of her when I was far younger, her diminutive frame and shock of white hair protesting the Lawrence government's refusal to hand back the old Swan Brewery site to Noongar people, for whom it is a sacred site. At the time, I didn't grasp the importance of the protest, but this image (possibly in the *West Australian*) showed me there was no such thing as a 'typical' activist.

Sipping at the first of many cups of earl grey, I was drawn to some of the titles wedged into a small bookcase in her spartan lounge. Eliot, Rilke, Wright, Heidegger, Meister Eckhart—all heavy hitters! But, like Veronica herself, they were there to invite, not to intimidate. In the next two hours we criss-crossed Western literature and thought, pausing only for my frantic scribbling (how do you spell 'Ricoeur'?) and her wonderful excoriations of economic rationalism and the delusions of 'our fantasy society'. Wright was her exemplar for how poetry must be corporeal, located within and felt through the body. The metaphysical without the physical risked pointless, even *dangerous*, abstraction. The desire for money was singled out as an abstraction separating people from their historical and environmental realities, and thus their innate responsibilities to them. What of Francis Webb, I asked, compared to Judith Wright? Veronica was instantly away. They knew each other's work of course, shared the same concerns, but Webb composes with whole histories of words, time collapsing under the strain. Wright does it too, but more freely, and much more in the body. Both liked their mystics, she added, all the greats do. Have you read St John of the Cross? Mystic *and* poet. How well do you know *Four Quartets*?[3] As we wound up, she gave me her copy of Antonella Riem Natale's new book *The One Life: Coleridge and Hinduism*.[4]

Veronica's parting advice was 'Keep your tin hat on'. This was much far more than a charge to 'stick with it'. By this point, in the late Howard years when his blatant anti-intellectualism had extended from fierce university cuts to open conflict with respected historians,

---

3. TS Eliot, *Four Quartets* (London: Faber, 2001).
4. Antonella Riem Natale, *The One Life: Coleridge and Hinduism* (Jaipur: Rawat, 2005).

I felt she was saying: 'The blows will come, but what you're doing matters more, and those who understand this get you support you.' As an Arts undergraduate, I had always relished how my 'economically irrational' degree baffled those who worshipped Doing Law or The Mines. Yet, for Veronica, theirs was the conspiracy: it was we literary types who were perfectly normal and justified in every way, ancient and modern. A few years later, at the first Two Tribes Poetry Festival in Braidwood, near Canberra, I saw her holding court in a large hall, hand on hip. 'Right', she began. 'I'm an elder now, so I'm going to say what I think and you can listen.' As a fledgling scholar, the exhilaration of having someone like this in your corner intellectually, emotionally, was simply incredible—but she also made you feel it was the basic right of every inquiring mind to be welcomed, respected, uplifted, believed.

Veronica never mentioned her own Christian mysticism scholarship. My PhD, which would later become *Christian Mysticism and Australian Poetry*[5] drew on *South of My Days*, *A Crucible of Prophets*[6] and her 1996 meditation on Reconciliation *Can These Bones Live?*[7] Yet ultimately her small 1974 book *The Mystics*[8] proved the more vital. Across its unassuming thirty-eight pages, *The Mystics* recounts Brady's attempt to understand Christian mysticism, beginning with her own admission 'Here I was, a supposed Christian, a religious [sic], professionally supposed to know about prayer. But I didn't know about mysticism, was even perhaps a little sceptical about it.'[9] Rather than tie herself in knots in what Grace M Jantzen calls 'the stately dance claims and counterclaims about experience and interpretation, language and ineffability'[10] which has echoed down the twentieth century since William James' *The Varieties of Religious Experience*[11], Brady instead engages with others at a commune in Geraldton, all

---

5. Toby Davidson, *Christian Mysticism and Australian Poetry* (New York: Cambria Press, 2013).
6. Veronica Brady, *A Crucible of Prophets: Australians and the Question of God* (Sydney: Theological Explorations, 1981).
7. Veronica Brady, *Can These Bones Live?* (Annandale: Federation, 1996).
8. Veronica Brady, *The Mystics* (East Malvern: Dove, 1974).
9. Brady, *The Mystics*, 8.
10. Grace M Jantzen, *Power, Gender and Christian Mysticism*. (Cambridge: Cambridge University Press, 1995), 3.
11. William James, *The Varieties of Religious Experience: A Study in Human Nature*, 1902. (Harmondsworth: Penguin, 1982).

identified by first name only with a little information about their edu-
cational background. In dialogues which reminded me of my own
Nedlands 'chat', the range is immense: Maharishi Maresh Yogi, transcendental meditation, quantum physics, St Paul, Buddha, contemporary music, Pythagoras, Descartes, Newton, Thomas à Kempis, Blake
(thrice), Wordsworth, Eliot, St Augustine, religion scholar Robert
Zachner, Jesus, Charles Manson, Eliot, a range of medieval mystics
from St Francis to St John of the Cross and Blaise Pascal, a few Prot-
estants including Henry Vaughan, then Amnesty International, Gan-
dhi, Martin Luther King, Camillo Torres, Bonhoeffer, Solzhenitsyn,
Thomas Merton, St Ignatius of Loyola and WH Auden.

For Brady, as for many mystics (not that I would dare designate
her such), the contemplative and active lives—the Mary-Martha dyad
of Luke 10:38–42—entirely cohere. This is obvious in Brady's own life,
but it is also evident in the figures she highlights in *The Mystics* as per-
sonally important. English mystic Julian of Norwich[12] is 'a favourite
of mine . . . I was always moved, too, by the vision she had in which
God showed her "everything that is, as it were, in the littleness of a
hazel nut, resting in his hand"'.[13] Her inclusion in Eliot's *Four Quartets*, written during the Blitz when Julian's small church was bombed
and, for Brady, 'the whole world seemed to be going down in flames'
lends a twentieth century resonance. The German theologian and
Nazi resistor Dietrich Bonhoeffer is also remarked upon at length:

> If mysticism means preoccupation with God as source
> and centre of my begin, if mysticism means prayer, then
> Bonhoeffer is offering a new model of mysticism for our
> times, one in which God is found not in the desert or in the
> hermitage, but in the midst of the city, even perhaps in the
> prison cell. And there is, after all, nothing impossible in that.[14]

A 'light bulb' moment in the writing of my thesis came when I realised
that Christian mysticism, and even more so Christian mystical poetry
(for example the non-Christian Judith Wright's 'Grace'[15] or Francis

---

12. Julian of Norwich, *Revelations of Divine Love*, translated by Clifton Wolters
    (Harmondsworth: Penguin, 1976).
13. Brady, *The Mystics*, 31.
14. Brady, *The Mystics*, 35.
15. Judith Wright, *Collected Poems 1942–1985* (Pymble. Angus & Robertson, 1994).

Webb's 'The Canticle'[16]) where subject to shifting definitions across time. This mean that 'mysticism' in 1902 was not the 'mysticism' of 2002. For William James, poets such as Wordsworth and Whitman were paradigm mystics, while for the current seminal historian of Christian mysticism, Bernard McGinn[17], such notions are highly dubious, though he does accept Blake as a 'great independent'.[18] No Australian scholar had explicitly noted shifting notions of mysticism (though it is implicit in Kevin Hart's *The Trespass of the Sign*[19]) and international scholars such as McGinn only gesture towards it. Brady went closer than anyone, and much earlier too, by asserting what mysticism *does* is more concrete than its conceptual mutations:

> What did it matter whether I could define the kinds of mysticism and trace out the various stages of the ascent to God, the purgative, the illuminative and the unitive ways? What matters finally is that state of silence, simplicity and humility the great mystics achieve and its effect on them and on all those with whom they come in to contact which renders them loving, compassionate and prepare to give themselves entirely for others.[20]

As ever, her logos, ethos and pathos are indistinguishable: the Aristotelian division of argument was not to be found in Sister Veronica Brady. Those who lift you up from nothing are the great ones indeed. She was brilliant and she was bloody tough too. I suspect I am not the only one still with my tin hat on.

---

16. Francis Webb, *Collected Poems* Toby Davidson, editor (Crawley: University of Western Australia, 2011).
17. Bernard McGinn, editor *The Essential Writings of Christian Mysticism* (New York: Modern Library, 2006).
18. James, *The Varieties of Religious Experience*, 299.
19. Kevin Hart, *The Trespass of the Sign: Deconstruction, Theology and Philosophy* (Cambridge: Cambridge University Press, 1989).
20. Brady, *The Mystics*, 40.

The Truth about Stories: Veronica Brady's Enduring Student Legacy

Angeline O'Neill

Not long ago I attended a Professional Development day for Humanities staff at a well-known tertiary institution. I am sure you know the sort of thing; an invited speaker from 'over east' armed with endless print outs of endless pie-charts and diagrams, the purpose of which is apparently to convince us of the indisputable relevance bordering on absolute necessity of other pie-charts and diagrams. (It is all evidence-based.)

I think it was somewhere between the fifth chart and the third Venn diagram that my attention began to wander and I found myself wondering if this is what academia is *really* about? Is this what it means? Why do we bother and why do our students bother? Of course, if I accept the basic premise of the Professional Development day, the answer is simple and obvious: employability, that's the name of the game.

Or is it? As important as this is, I believe academia is so much more.

I guess I had a bit of a Virginia Woolf moment, when in *A Room of One's Own* Mary Beton lets her thoughts drift. You might remember that Mary is sitting on a riverbank in the grounds of the euphemistically titled Oxbridge University, thinking about a paper she has been asked to give on women and fiction. This quickly becomes a meditation on the meaning of words:

> . . . at second sight the words seemed not so simple . . . I should never be able to come to a conclusion. I should never be able to fulfil what is, I understand, the first duty of a lecturer—to

hand you after an hour's discourse a nugget of pure truth to
wrap up between the pages of your notebooks and keep on the
mantelpiece for ever.[1]

What, I wondered, is the relationship between words, 'nuggets of
pure truth' and notebooks? What, I wondered, inspires passion borne
of academic curiosity; that which I see in and share with my students?
Perhaps it is a fascination with the extraordinary power of words
(whether spoken or written) and the process of storying. Perhaps we
seek to understand the nature of knowledge and truth? Perhaps it's
the way that we are all protagonists in our own stories and we question where our stories fit in a wider context. What is the aim of our
story: the plot, the meaning and of course, the ending? Perhaps it's a
little of each of these.

So it was that, as I stared out the window into High Street, I found
myself thinking about Veronica Brady.

I knew Veronica in various capacities: as her last PhD student;
as an academic at a Catholic institution the establishment of which
she vigorously opposed; and she was also godmother to our daughter,
Dara.

So her effect on me was both academic and personal. In fact, the
better I knew her the more inextricably linked these elements became.

But perhaps I should backtrack a little. I first met Veronica when
I was fresh off a plane from Sydney, having just finished my Honours
year at Sydney University and having accepted a scholarship to study
Australian literature at the University of Western Australia. Unfortu-
nately, I had already forgotten whether I had just crossed the continent to do a Masters or a PhD—in any case, it didn't really matter as
I had no idea what either of them involved. I was shown to her office
in the Faculty of Arts by a secretary who advised me in hushed tones
'just don't call her *Sister* Veronica . . . she hates it'.

Trepidation.

And there I was, standing in front of her desk. She looked up from
whatever she had been writing.

'Sit down', she said, looking over the top of her glasses at me with a
frown and paradoxically, the faintest of smiles. 'Angeline, a PhD is an

---

1.   Virginia Woolf, *A Room of One's Own* (London: Vintage, 1996), 3.

original contribution to the body of knowledge.' She paused dramatically. 'What's yours?'

I was, of course, gob-smacked. Thirty seconds previously I hadn't even known what a PhD was, never mind what the earth shattering outcome of mine would be. (Incidentally, I have ensured that I have never said the same thing to any of my own doctoral students.) It was a challenging not to say inauspicious start to a journey I believe I'll continue for the rest of my life.

It is an understatement to say that for the first two years of my PhD Veronica was definitely not my favourite person. She hovered around with a critical, challenging, even pedantic eye—or so I thought—as I pursued Englishman EL Grant Watson, mapping his Australian journeys through his fiction and non-fiction. The more I persevered the more interested and interesting she became and the more stimulating were our meetings. She was given to paradoxical statements, the meaning of which often didn't strike me for several weeks. I remember her saying that I had a habit of stumbling onto ideological minefields. On another occasion, when I bemoaned my obtuseness, she readily agreed but added that 'we are all obtuse sometimes'. Later, she simply stated that 'we must learn to think scientifically about unscientific things'. This gave me food for thought.

In Veronica I saw someone who valued critical thinking more than anyone I had previously known. She was never afraid to express her views and always prepared to support them. Her passion throughout life for social justice and her belief in a better world through our thoughts, words and actions was nothing short of inspirational. No 'nuggets of pure truth' to be wrapped in notebooks and admired from afar. Just words. *Just* words? A knowledge of their power for good and ill is an enduring legacy, particularly when in the minds and hearts of students. Such is Veronica's legacy; not only for those of us who were fortunate enough to have her as a supervisor or lecturer, but also our own students; for example, at the university where I am employed we offer a unit entitled *Freedom From Oppression*, which deals with the role of the written and spoken word as a form of both freedom and oppression.

Whenever students have what I call a 'light bulb moment' in one of these classes and you can see they are thinking a thought they've never had before, I see evidence of what I've already described as passion for social justice and a belief in a better world through our thoughts, words and actions. So too, when former students who are now university lecturers in their own right, or secondary school teachers or primary teachers contact me for lecture summaries and references, because they are including a text from these units in their own classes, I see something of Veronica's enduring legacy; her refusal to accept the way things are just because that's the way they have always been.

Not everything can be understood, however. Academics of all people should know this, and Veronica knew it very well. If her belief in the achievement of a better world was inspirational, so was her reverence for the unknown and unknowable. In fact, in an essay entitled 'It's All in the Unfolding', she remarks that

> I have always had a sense of mystery, unknown, of some reality beyond my own projections, which nevertheless leaves its trace on them, a reality that can be subversive and can interrupt my plans in a way that is both painful and pleasurable since it calls me to go further, to challenge the pain of things in the name of a love, justice and understanding which it is our responsibility to achieve.[2]

Of course, Veronica was a great story teller; from her rigorous academic works to her opinion pieces to her casual dinner time conversation. She knew the value of a story, whether it be academic research or the story my then three-year old daughter told of a conversation she had had with the gum tree in Veronica's courtyard at the aptly named Gum Tree House. This story was treated with the utmost respect (probably more so than many journal articles she encountered) and Veronica often referred to it in later years.

Well, in telling something of Veronica's story, I've told you part of my own narrative now. That's how stories work. In retrospect I realise that the aforementioned Professional Development day was in fact of great value, although not for the reasons intended by the organisers. (I remain sceptical of the necessity for pie-charts and Venn diagrams in all Humanities lectures.) Nevertheless, as I stared out the window

---

2. Veronica Brady, 'It's All in the Unfolding', in *Carrying the Banner: Women, Leadership and Activism in Australia*, edited by Joan Eveline and Lorraine Hayden (Crawley: University of Western Australia Press, 1999), 217–223. Many thanks to Dr Dominic Hyde for sending me a copy of this chapter.

during the presentation, I occupied a time and space in which to contemplate why I do what I do: privileged to be a member of an academic community, a researcher and perhaps most importantly, a teacher. It's not just a job, it's central to who and what I am—I suspect you know what I mean. It's part of my story; a story into which Veronica Brady came cycling on her beloved bicycle, Xavier, in 1991 with a glass of cabernet sauvignon in one hand and a tattered copy of Miguel de Cervantes' *Don Quixote* in the other.

Had she ever had the opportunity to meet Cherokee writer Thomas King, she would have liked him very much, and I believe her total disregard of authority for its own sake would have appealed to him. In his collection of Massey lectures, entitled *The Truth About Stories: a Native Narrative*, King writes:

> I tell the stories not to play on your sympathies but to suggest how stories can control our lives, for there is a part of me that has never been able to move past these stories, a part of me that will be chained to these stories as long as I live . . .[3]

After all, he continues, 'the truth about stories is that's all we are.'[4]

I believe Veronica and Tom would have agreed on this.

---

3. Thomas King, *The Truth About Stories: A Native Narrative* (Toronto: House of Anansi Press, 2003), 9.
4. King, *The Truth About Stories*, 62.

A Forum for a Theology in the World Vol 4 No 1&2/2017

Dinner at Loreto

Terri-Ann White

My testimony is all about care and community. I was straight out of university, after a detour in rock and roll entrepreneurship: wild nights and risky behaviour. At twenty-three, because in those days BA degrees could last as long as you wanted them to, I opened a bookshop in Perth. A bookshop full of books I was interested in—one of those rare enterprises where self-interest works. Through my role as owner and operator of this bookshop, I was initiated into another world: of ideas, passion, politics and commitment to a personal ethics of care and responsibility. I became friends with many women who were a generation or more ahead of me, who trusted me in their circles and their lives—women who were politicians, policy makers, activists; leaders in this society, artists and cultural commissars.

That was how I met Veronica Brady, or VB to many of her cheeky friends. On the hustings, as it were; talking about books and ideas, on protest rallies, in shouty meetings of contestation, and then at dinners at Loreto. I recognise how lucky I was at the time. I had access to and friendship with people I would describe as small-m mentors, unfettered access, intimate insights, trust. I was always the youngest person in the room, in the gathering. Now, at fifty-seven, I continue many of these regular meetings with my influential mentors, meetings conducted over wine and food usually: convivial, pleasurable, providing the backbone to the sort of life I chose for myself. Many of those choices came through these experiences in my twenties and thirties. They are the formative ones for me as a woman who made her own family through friendships that last a lifetime.

The dinners at Loreto were unusual at first. I had no experience of religion, really, not since I was confirmed at my school because I had a crush on the Anglican priest and desired more time talking to him. All strictly in the realm of *the life of the mind.* To enter the convent was startling in its ordinariness. The large kitchen was impressive, and the women who prepared our food were very capable. As I had grown up living in hotels, I was not alarmed at this division of labour. The food was semi-institutional, but in those days Australian cuisine was a bit like that anyway. I don't remember how many of these dinners I attended; it may have only been three. But each had a different set of women in attendance. On two occasions I recall that a woman, university connected, who had experienced life-changing trauma, was invited. She was barely verbal and very withdrawn from the vivacity at the table. Veronica had the ability to allow her to sit there, share a meal, not speak but also not freak out, and it was clear that VB had returned her to the world of the social, as I expect she had been doing for this woman for the decades since the trauma that destroyed her family. I liked that hands-off approach—that was one, I like to think, that I paid attention to and stored away for later.

No topics—as far as I could see—were off limits at Loreto. Perhaps I am naïve in saying it, but that was my impression of those heady days upstairs at Loreto, and I'm sure many people in this [Symposium] room can attest to this, fuelled as they were by Veronica's favourite, all varietals of red wine.

Later, when Veronica moved to her beloved Gum Tree House to live independently, a solution was smoothly, silently, and effectively found by her friends who wished to continue the pleasurable experience of dinner with Veronica. You see, the first time we attended dinner there, the food was a little idiosyncratic. VB had some unusual ideas about menus for guests and, to be honest, was more adept at reading and critical thinking than cooking for up to eight guests. The system changed swiftly and each dish for any proposed dinner was supplied by a guest—in consultation with the other guests, and Veronica was reinstated as host rather than cook. (I could tell you about the warm fish milkshake, but I promised myself I wouldn't.)

I missed the late dinners in VB's life: my working life at The University of Western Australia became all-consuming for years and I missed out on much. But Veronica's role as a colleague, a friend, one always up for verbal jousting, a role model and a mentor won't be forgotten. She initiated me by example into the world of hospitality and the abiding friendships between women.

A Forum for a Theology in the World Vol 4 No 1&2/2017

Travels with Veronica Brady, Dante and Cervantes

Christine Choo

A long time ago, in another country that was the 1970s, Sister Veronica Brady IBVM, PhD, came to Perth, Western Australia, to teach at the university here. She was spirited, adventurous and fiercely independent. Being the good Catholic nun that she was, Veronica soon found her way to the Chaplaincy service at the university where she met like-minded Catholics and Jesuit priest and Catholic chaplain, Father John Harte, who gathered weekly to celebrate Mass together as a group they named 'Ecclesia' (from the Greek, *ekklesia* or church). It was here that I met Veronica. It was here, among like-minded friends and a supportive community, that our commitment to social justice, the preferential option for the poor and sound exegesis were nurtured. Veronica remained linked with Ecclesia until the group formally disbanded not long before she moved into the MercyCare Aged Care hostel in Wembley when she was no longer able to live independently. Other members of Ecclesia, by then grandparents like myself, were still in contact with each other and with Veronica.

Monday afternoons at MercyCare were precious to Veronica and me. Our conversations would wander to wherever Veronica took them, chatting about the various books piled on the table in her room or the pictures, including her favourite Leunig cartoons, that she cut out and pasted on the walls to keep herself amused, or about the lovely roses she had just picked from the hostel garden. We talked about her beloved family, her travels and adventures in Italy, Spain and other places. We would soon settle into the focus of the afternoon as we sat on the terrace or patio in summer or by a window with a view to the garden in winter. Then we would take turns to read aloud Veronica's favourite version, Allen Mendelbaum's translation, of Dante Alighieri's *The Divine Comedy*, which had both the original Italian and the English on facing pages.

Veronica convinced me that we should start at *Purgatorio* because *Inferno* was 'too gruesome and depressing'. We would read a few Cantos at each session, stopping to admire Dante's imagery, cosmology, metaphor, turn of phrase or references to interesting people in unfamiliar contexts. We went on this wonderful journey twice, the second time starting from the beginning, in *Inferno*. We came to the conclusion that Dante's mystical insight and vision of Heaven (God's presence) left him in awe, unable to fully describe his experience of it.

From time to time Veronica would launch into a recital, in the original Italian, of her favourite passage, in which Dante's beloved muse Beatrice brings him to the threshold of Paradise (*Paradiso*, Canto 1, 103–142). These impromptu recitations were always wonderfully expressive.

> All things, among themselves,
> possess an order, and this order is
> the form that makes the universe like God.
> Here do the higher beings see the imprint
> of the Eternal Worth, which is the end
> to which the pattern I have mentioned tends.
> Within that order, every nature has
> its bent, according to different station,
> nearer or less near to its origin.
> Therefore, these natures move to different ports
> across the might sea of being, each
> given the impulse that will bear it on.
> This impulse carries fire to the moon;
> this is the motive force in mortal creatures;
> this binds the earth together, makes it one.
> *Paradiso*, Canto I, 103–114

After we had read *The Divine Comedy* for the second time, when we were casting about for our next read, Veronica readily jumped at the opportunity to read Robinson Smith's 1914 translation of Cervantes' literary marvel, *Don Quijote de La Mancha*. I suspect that the thought of reading the hundred-year-old translation whetted her appetite for it. Again, we took turns to read passages from this most entertaining and insightful work, chuckling as we read, commenting on the social context and crazy situations that Don Quijote got himself into with his horse Rocinante, and his trusted Sancho Panza and his donkey. The adventures of the deluded Knight Errant and his level headed assistant kept us entertained and chatting for weeks, as we plumbed the depths of this work.

> In a village of La Mancha, whose name I do not care to recall, there lately lived one of those gentlemen that keep a lance in the rack, an ancient shield, a rake of a horse and one lone harrier-hound. A stew of rather more beef than mutton, usually appearing at supper as a salad, lentils Friday, tripe and trouble, Saturday and young pigeon as a delicacy on Sunday, relieved him of three-fourths of his income; whilst a doublet of broadcloth with velvet breeches and slippers for feast-days and a week-day livery of the finest homespun made away with the rest. His family comprised a housekeeper past forty, a niece under twenty and a yokel for field and mart, who saddled the nag as nimbly as he handled the pruning-hook. The age of our hidalgo bordered on fifty years, but though dry of visage and spare of flesh he boasted a vigorous constitution, was a great early-riser and a lover of the chase.
> *Don Quixote*, opening lines of Chapter 1

When we reached the end of Book 1 of *Don Quijote*, Veronica decided that we should not go on to read Book 2 just yet. We had discussed the possibility of reading Toni Morrison's *O Mercy*, just for something completely different. But this was not to be. Veronica died a few days after we completed Book 1 of *That Imaginative Gentleman Don Quijote de La Mancha*.

It has been such a pleasure and privilege to travel with Veronica and her companions, Dante and Cervantes, and to enjoy the insights, memories, conversations, laughter, quirky sense of humour and fun we shared on these travels. We were from time to time in the company of Beatrice and Dulcinea del Tobosa, Virgil and Sancho Panza, and others of good and ill repute. We marvelled at the Universe, visited innumerable inns, tilted at windmills, fought the enemy, came upon familiar characters in unfamiliar contexts and went to Hell and back. Reading Dante and Cervantes connected Veronica to her former life; it touched her heart, and it gave her a little spark to the end.

Thank you Veronica, my friend, for sharing these adventures.

Brady and Intellectual Belief

Dark Places: The Movement of the Image (Thoughts on the work of Veronica Brady)*

Gail Jones

Fra Angelico's painting, *Pious Women at the Tomb* (1440), depicts four tragically bewildered women looking for the absent body of Christ. One holds her hand at her brow like an explorer, and is peering down into his marble casket as into a vastly deep well. Three others stand by, sadly dumfounded. Behind the women, floating in air, is an image of the risen Christ, autonomous, autotelic, blazing in a mystical disc. But the women all look the wrong way and are left bereft. An angel points to the vision, but still their gaze is misdirected. A Dominican monk kneels in reverence before the empty space; a passage of gospel script instructs as to the correct sign to read; still, the four women stare into darkness.

---

* Reprinted with kind permission from *Coolabah* (forthcoming 2017).

The image, one might say, is essentially of *mistake*: of assuming emptiness and absence, and of missing meaning. The image asks, what is the remainder of any death? How might secure significance be made? What signs offer consolation; what *immaterially* might make sense?

Bruno Latour uses this image, among others, to make a distinction between idolatry and iconophilia: idolatry he defines as giving entire attention to the visual, as if this might offer unmediated access to the truth; iconophilia, on the other hand, 'respects . . . not the image, but the movement of the image'; it respects 'the series of transformations for which each image is only a provisional frame'.[1] This distinction is relevant beyond the art-historical: it is an example of including what we might call an 'inferred' dimension, generously and openly, in all forms of knowledge—in science, philosophy, art and social theory. Science, in particular, can learn from art. Latour recommends 'multiplying mediators', so that in our understandings, as in our readings of paintings, we consider movements of disembodiment and re-embodiment, we imagine competing vectors in the construction of meaning, we admit the non-realist and inexact qualities in all things. Latour uses obdurate terms like 'information transfer' to describe the circuitry of Fra Angelico's painting, but he's moved by its indirection and complication, and believes too that these are the basis for reconstructing an open model of knowledge. The woman with her hand to her brow, peering into enigma, is emblematic of the limit of material—let us say, *positivist*—signs; yet also human, deeply human, in the intensity of her searching.

*

Iconophilic in Bruno Latour's sense, much of Veronica Brady's intellectual life worked with the principles of Fra Angelico's vision: the negotiation of puzzled being, the deep mystery of invisible presence, the ways in which art speaks in oblique and multiple registers. Peering into the darkness. Intuiting, not seeing directly. The human condition of stranded yearning after unverifiable transcendence.

---

1. Bruno Latour 'How to be Iconophilic in Art, Science and Religion', in *Picturing Science, Producing Art*, edited by Peter Gallison and Caroline A Jones (London: Psychology Press, 1998), 418–30; 421. See also Adam S Miller, *Speculative Grace: Bruno Latour and Object Orientated Theology* (New York: Fordham University Press, 2013).

Veronica spoke robustly of '*the idol of the answer*'.[2] She considered questions to be much more important than answers and her manner, though often publically hyper-declarative, was more privately, and more secretly, interrogative. When she chose her name as a Loreto sister—*Veronica*—the attraction was in part to a flimsy, even uncertain vision, and the idea of bearing of witness to physical suffering. She disdained sentimentalism, but was engaged by the charm of imagery. And in her own case, the idea of contact with the holy that was at once physical and metaphysical. The *trace*, a notion she loved, seemed to her to say something essential about how we apprehend mystery and are in a necessary relation of existential humility to the larger dramas of the world.

---

2. I was reminded of this phrase when I saw Veronica cited in Gareth Griffiths' 'Open Spaces, Contested Places: Writing and the Fundamentalist Inscription of Territory', in *Writing Fundamentalism*, edited by Axel Stähler and Klaus Stierstorfer (**Newcastle upon Tyne:** Cambridge Scholars, 2009), 58.

The so-called 'Master of Saint Veronica' produced this image in about 1420, 'St Veronica and the Sudarium', showing a modest and lovely woman holding up a gigantic Christ head on a veil. Now in the National Gallery in London, I lodge on this painting among the many perhaps because its proportions are so endearingly odd and its saint's face so endearingly distinctive.

*

Veronica Brady's heterodoxy centred on the *trace*. The undoing of certainty, *kenosis* as a mode of knowing: these were the cherished principles of her own version of faith. Her commitment to Australian literature was defined by essentially religious questions—but not doctrinally so (indeed she was ferociously anti-doctrinal), rather by the manner in which imaginative life produces and contemplates images of being and nothingness. Drawn to the symbolic, she was devoted in particular to the work of Patrick White, whom she held to be *sui generis* (her term) and paradigmatic.

The material/immaterial nexus, so central to White's imagining, was for Veronica Brady a touchstone to her own theology. She spoke sincerely of his work as a 'theological training', even as she described the writer himself as cranky, mischievous and sometimes perversely cruel. Further, she wrote of White as engaged in 'saintly' narrative and like the Jewish theologian Edith Wyschogrod, a congenial influence in her later years, the heuristic terms *narrativity, corporeality, textuality* and *historicality* were the basis for reading as moral philosophy.[3] Citing both *Saints and Postmodernism* and *An Ethics of Remembering*,[4] she found in these books an eclecticism not unlike her own, and a philosophical preoccupation with similar themes.

The central concern was antique and inveterate: the question of literature as a vehicle for spiritual values. But so too, and crucially, was the matter of ideology. In Australia Veronica Brady was a public figure of leftist politics and a fearless activist, aware of the econ-

---

3. Edith Wyschogrod, *Saints and Postmodernism: Revisioning Moral Philosophy* (Chicago: Chicago University Press, 1990), 5.
4. Edith Wyschogrod, *An Ethics of Remembering: History, Heterology and the Nameless Others* (Chicago: Chicago University Press, 1998). Wyschgorod was a scholar principally of Levinas, but also dealt with many other thinkers, Heidegger, Derrida, Deleuze and Sloterdijik among them, and connected themes of alterity, catastrophe and the need for regeneration of the spirit.

omy within which power accrues to the privileged and the wealthy. Her sympathies were radical, with the disenfranchised, the dispossessed, the neglected and the suffering; and religious vocation was the ineluctable centre of her values. Liberation theology, Simone Weil, the work of philosophers who dealt with the idea that meaning might be beyond fixity (like Derrida),[5] her Nietzschean conviction that the present age requires a 'transvaluation of values'[6]—these were the essential fixtures of her intellectual life. How valiant a thinker, and how principled. How bold and impertinent in her hermeneutical heterogeneity. I'm reminded here of Roland Barthes: 'the critic does not ask to be granted a "vision" or a "style", but only to be granted the right to a certain discourse, which is an *indirect discourse*.'[7] Those who knew Veronica hear her voice in her prose and recognise the strenuous practice of a particular discourse. She possessed key terms and notions; but was always alert to new theories and difficult ideas, so that the epistemological grounds of her argument were flexible, variable and sometimes also a little vague.

Veronica's championing of the cause of indigenous Australians (and their literature) is well known.[8] Apart from the wish to honour and make known Aboriginal writing, she wanted also to accuse, to express dismay, and to insist on white culpability. Settler Australia, she maintained, was *constitutively* racist and founded on an anxious drama of psychogeography:

> The way most settlers then and now chose to deal with it [frontier violence], was to deny their situation and repress any sense of guilt, projecting it instead outwards, onto their victims. In this way . . . the Aborigine came to be figured as the Wild Man, the embodiment not only of all that is savage, that

---

5. John D Caputo's *The Tears and Prayers of Jacques Derrida: Religion without Religion* (Bloomington, IN: Indiana University Press, 1997) was one of Veronica's favourite books.

6. This was her often-used phrase. Veronica agreed with Nietzsche's critique of institutional Christianity as in some ways decadent, corrupt and in need of reform.

7. Roland Barthes, *Critical Essays* (Northwestern University Press, 1972), translated by Robert Howard, xii.

8. See for example the essays in her *Caught in the Draught: On Contemporary Australian Culture and Society* (Angus and Robertson, 1994). This volume includes essays on Mabo, Bill Neidjie, and indigenous writing more generally.

is uncivilized, but also evil. Psychologically, this projection was helpful. After the trauma of leaving home and the long, difficult and dangerous voyage and, faced with an equally difficult and dangerous environment, the precise content of their own humanity no longer seemed clear. But at least they could assure themselves they were 'not like that', like the Aborigines.[9]

Versions of this argument appear throughout her work. Most telling here is the phrase 'Psychologically, this projection was useful'. Indebted initially to Jung (whom she later fiercely repudiated), she relied mostly on a naturalized Freudian lexicon—repression, projection, sublimation; also the use-value, as it were, of certain forms of displacement. Unusually perhaps for a Catholic thinker, she also located evil in self-interested projection and alienation and deplored the cultural capital possessed by those whom, with a wry and canny smile, she liked to call 'the pseudo-religious'. Her models were White's characters—the banal and platitudinous Mrs Flack and Mrs Jolly from *Riders in the Chariot,* Mr and Mrs Merrivale in *The Fringe of Leaves;* the smugly ignorant Mr Bonner in *Voss*.[10] Bonner, the financier of Voss's journey, was a man who 'was inclined to jingle his money in his pocket, for fear that he might find himself still apprenticed to the past';[11] this tiny detail also draws attention to the allegiance of capitalism and colonialism and the deathly fetish of money Veronica saw everywhere in action. One of her articles was entitled 'Polyphonies of Self';[12] the metaphor of White's autopoesis of faceted flaws is referenced here; likewise her belief that monoculture is fascistic and that self must be grounded in multiplicity. She was fond of quoting particular passages which made clear the false consciousness and anxiety of those who are spiritually afraid:

> Safe in life, safe in death, the merchant [Bonner] liked to feel. In consequence, he had often tried to calculate, for how much and from whom, salvation might be bought and, to ensure his

---

9. Quoted in Alma Buderlean, *Otherness in the Novels of Patrick White* (Peter Lang, 2007), 128.
10. Veronica Brady, 'God, History and Patrick White', in *Antipodes*, 19/2 (2005): 172–6.
11. Patrick White, *Voss* (Penguin, 1983), 17.
12. This is in Brady's *Caught in the Draught*, 30–7.

last entrance would be made through the last cedar door, had
begun in secret to subscribe liberal sums to all denominations,
including those of which he approved.[13]

Mystery is that which is incalculable and which has no profit, or sum.
Convinced of the Manichean allegory,[14] Veronica saw in White's satir-
ical portrait of colonial mentality a broader social diagnosis of mis-
taken value. Those who see only material signs are stranded in a
depleted symbolic order.

Patrick White wearing the wooden cross Veronica had given him

*

Against status, wealth, the comfortable life, Veronica recommended
spiritual and intellectual 'discomfort'. Although she called herself a
'social-materialist', she believed the immaterial, generally speaking,
to have vital energy and agency and was enthralled to both the escha-
tological and mystical promise of the numinous. Materiality itself
depends on invisible entities, of which consciousness, the innerness
that incessantly moves outward, is the human sign; and mysticism is

---

13. Patrick White, *Voss*, 349.
14. See Abdul R JanMohamed, *Manichean Aesthetics: the Politics of Literature in
    Colonial Africa* (University of Massachusetts Press, 1983).

the glorious possibility of transcendental semiosis. Theologically, it is *interception* that defines the link. Not will. Not desire. Not spiritual practice or enterprise. Veronica often cited David Marr's account of Patrick White's fall into the muck on his farm at Castle Hill, cursing the God he did not believe in then being 'interrupted . . . by a grandeur too overwhelming to express'.[15] Loss of freedom, abjection, unconcealment, a crucially transvaluing shift in scale: these were the forms of a true epiphany. In the *via negativa* tradition to which Veronica was allied, it was Stan Parker's loneliness at the end of *The Tree of Man*, during which he spits into the dirt at the feet of an evangelist, the complicated suffering of the four elect outcasts in *Riders in the Chariot*, Elizabeth Hunter's Lear-like unmaking and dissolution in *The Eye of the Storm*, that offered moments of philosophical instruction. One might say these were the icons of her Australian model of faith. 'In White's work', she wrote, 'discomfort rather than comfort is the sign of God's presence'.[16] That she matched her Christian sensibility to his image repertoire does not mean she was wholly uncritical; but certainly she considered White a theologian of sorts.

Even more than discomfort, Veronica believed in what she nominated 'the darkness of God'. If one must simply endure, and wait on interception, then religion, like interpretation, must submit to contingency and over-determined possibility. She was among the first critics to notice how profoundly White's writing relied on images of light and darkness. Writing on Ellen Roxburgh, captive of Aborigines in colonial Australia in *The Fringe of Leaves*, she suggests:

> Women perhaps know more of this darkness, bodily as well as socially . . . Women's bodily existence makes us more aware of our own finitude and of our subjection to physical necessity, more aware of the need for the descent into the darkness of life if new life is to emerge.[17]

---

15. Veronica Brady, 'A Grandeur Too Overwhelming to Express: Patrick White's Vision of God', in *Faith and Freedom: Christian Ethics in a Pluralist Culture*, edited David Neville and Phillip Matthews, (Adelaide: Australian Theological Forum Press, 2003), 153.

16. Brady, 'A Grandeur Too Overwhelming to Express: Patrick White's Vision of God', 153.

17. Brady, 'A Grandeur Too Overwhelming to Express: Patrick White's Vision of God', 157.

Veronica has in mind here the moment of Ellen's cannibalism, constructed through motifs of communion and sanctification. That she endorses White's wish to make holiness of necessity is entirely within the frame they mutually recommend, an insistence that 'civilization' has a shadow side that might be the route to other forms of being and knowing. Careful to avoid primitivism or some 'use-value' casting of Aboriginal Australians into spiritual guides, both the critic and the writer risk the insidious implication that abjection is finally the measure of self-realisation—or what has been identified as the supplanting of indigenous rights and presence with that of the 'white indigene'.[18] What is interesting is the degree to which both are in concord; unfashionable spiritualism informs White's and Brady's vision of Australian meaning and neither resile from its vigorous defence. In part this was a critique of Australian secularism:

> Religion, it seems, is a scandal that refuses to go away, even in the most secular of societies . . . the impulse continues and must be acknowledged and lived through, especially perhaps in a secular society since it has to do with negative and midliminal experience . . . as common to the unbeliever as the believer.[19]

Unbelievers and believers alike are subject to the 'impulse' to recognize and assess 'negative' experience. When Veronica Brady located her own search in the field of Australian literary studies, she sought to affirm the study of language and narrative—and the movement of images—as an endeavour that might, with due humility, enter and know fields of darkness.

*

There are no adequate summaries of the lives or thoughts of others. There are no accounts possible of the histories of our deepest

---

18. See, for example, Karin Hansson, 'The Indigenous and the Metropolitan in *A Fringe of Leaves*', in *World Literature Written in English*, 24/1 (1984): 178–189; Penelope Ingram, 'Racializing Babylon: Settler Whiteness and the "New Racism"', in *New Literary History*, 32/1 (2001): 157–176; also Kay Schaffer's careful point of view analysis of the indigene in *A Fringe of Leaves* in *In the Wake of First Contact: the Eliza Fraser Stories* (Cambridge University Press 1995).
19. Brady, *Caught in the Draught*.

affections. Those we love remain illimitable, like the sky beyond the window. And inadequation (*the non-realist, the inexact*) is also the condition of bereavement: words are spoken, memories rehearsed, there are exchanges of sorts, there are even modest retrievals and small confirmations—'yes, I remember, yes, she once said that'— but the lost are always beyond, becoming stylized as we speak of them.

So it is the poetic, more properly *poesis,* to which I turn. Veronica adored poetry, above all that of Francis Webb, Rainer Maria Rilke and Wallace Stevens. A few lines of Stevens come to mind:

> Here, now, we forget each other and ourselves. We feel the obscurity of an order, a whole, A knowledge, that which arranged the rendezvous.

> Within its vital boundary, in the mind. We say God and the imagination are one . . . How high that highest candle lights the dark.[20]

For Veronica the idea that God is also the faculty of imagination is not sacrilegious, nor does it discount what she thought of as the utter alterity of her God. Another kind of modernist, Stevens considers the gentle, 'intensest rendezvous', not interception or interruption. Wallace's speaking voice is located in the calm repose of the dim room at dusk, feeling 'the obscurity of an order', apprehending settling presences; Veronica is equally attracted to a rougher vision and one emphatically local. There's another kind of indwelling and transfiguration—in the natural world, and in disorder. In *The Fringe of Leaves* we find this moment:

> There was an occasion when she fell down, scattering skywards a cloud of ashen parrots. She would have continued lying on the ground and perhaps become her true self: once the flesh melts, and the skeleton inside it is blessed with its final articulate white, amongst the stones, beneath the hard sky, in this country to which it can at last belong.[21]

---

20. Wallace Stevens, 'Final Soliloquy of the Eternal Paramour'.
21. Patrick White, *A Fringe of Leaves* (London: Jonathan Cape, 1976), 281.

All shadows are black. All bones are white. This other kind of white-ness, 'the final articulate white' of death. As far as I know Veronica never commented on this moment in her favourite novel. But it seems to me an apposite point at which to conclude the imagining of her imagining, and the giving of honour to her important, still-persisting work.

A Forum for a Theology in the World Vol 4 No 1&2/2017

Veronica Brady: A Most Curious Theist

Dominic Hyde

Veronica Brady, my Aunty Veronica—or 'Ronnie' as she was affectionately known in the family—was a most curious theist indeed. Her theism was curious to *her*, attested to by her many explorations within and beyond its accepted boundaries, and curious to *me*. Like Bertrand Russell, while agnostic I am effectively an atheist.[1] And it was Veronica who I first took as giving licence to my 'atheism'. When eleven or twelve years old, becoming bored with Sunday Mass and feeling no draw towards religion (despite my Jesuit schooling), it was Veronica who seemed to 'sanction' my disinterest (though, on reflection, it was the *institution* of religion I think she saw as the proper target). Over the following years I tried to understand her religious commitment but most attempts in conversation with her too quickly moved into surrounding matters. She left her theology undefended and largely unexplained as the conversation moved to a more secular discussion of her favourite issues invariably involving

---

1. Bertrand Russell, 'What is an Agnostic?', in *The Basic Writings of Bertrand Russell*, edited by Robert Egner and John Slater (London: Routledge, 2009), 556:

   > . . . an Agnostic may hold that the existence of God, though not impossible, is very improbable; he may even hold it so improbable that it is not worth considering in practice. In that case, he is not far removed from atheism. His attitude may be that which a careful philosopher would have towards the gods of ancient Greece. If I were asked to prove that Zeus and Poseidon and Hera and the rest of the Olympians do not exist, I should be at a loss to find conclusive arguments. An Agnostic may think the Christian God as improbable as the Olympians; in that case, he is, for practical purposes, at one with the atheists.

justice, goodness, tolerance and the transcendental. It was not that she was obviously evasive (and certainly not defensive—I have never known her to be defensive!). It seemed more as if she simply thought the current conversation was more interesting on these associated matters.

So my curiosity remained, heightened all the more by her frequent transgressions of Church doctrine. She revelled in the freedom afforded a woman in the Catholic Church (in particular the fact that she could not be stripped of holy orders which women were barred from receiving anyway). Her theism was more frequently noted in public by doctrinal breach rather than slavish accordance. Ours was a liberal-minded Catholic family to the extent that her liberation theology seemed the only respectable form of theology going, but it clearly strained at the boundaries of Catholicism for some. I remember a very conservative Catholic philosopher at The University of Western Australia, my undergraduate teacher at the time, outraged at the mere fact that I was her nephew. It was as if, through blood-ties, I had inherited her 'heretical thinking'. And this thinking so disturbed him that he declared that I would never succeed as an academic. (He himself was a 1950s émigré from Eastern Europe, fleeing the 'tyranny of irreligious Marxism', and took the view that some systems of belief, including Catholicism, were by their very nature unable to be taken as objects of critical scrutiny of the kind Veronica was engaged in without thereby making belief impossible. You just *couldn't* accept Catholicism *and* simultaneously subject it to the criticisms being levelled at it—his Catholicism was a 'closed belief system' as he put it. Veronica's liberation theology was a form of 'Catholic Marxism' and it was Marxism he had fled at considerable cost.) This helped sharpen my awareness of how unorthodox Veronica was to many fellow theists—there was a lot there that she rejected—but I still didn't really understand the positive component of Veronica's theism. If the Church was so wrong on so many crucial matters of justice, why be a theist at all?

In her more formal moments we do find her religious commitment more clearly exposed. For example, in her 1991 essay 'Intellectual Belief and Freedom', in the course of a broad discussion, she makes the following implicit argument in defence of the religious:

first, that a culture or society that takes no account of
the religious dimension, of a 'level of reality beyond the
observable world known to science, to which are ascribed
meaning and purposes completing and transcending those
of the purely human realm', is thereby impoverished; and
secondly that acceptance of this dimension, together with
sustained and careful thought about it, may be necessary to
preserve whatever it is that we mean by 'freedom'.[2]

She continues:

freedom [in the relevant sense] has to do with a habit of mind
rather than with institutions, since it describes an ability to
make choices for oneself. It is this ability that is at risk in our
society today, where, to draw on Habermas's analysis, System
tends to dominate Life-world. It would seem, therefore, that
domination ought to be the concern of intellectuals who
believe in freedom.[3]

Intellectual freedom is compromised by the domination of instrumental rationality that sees all as a means to the furtherance of our
currently-accepted economic and political structures (the System).
They are unexamined ends in themselves, leaving no room for open
questioning of the values inherent in and presupposed by these structures and their goals. Our horizons draw in, our Life-world narrows,
and we become dominated by a world-view that does not offer or
consider possible alternatives. We are dominated by its 'rationality'
and alternative choices are closed off from us. This Veronica rails
against. And quite rightly, in my view.

So can we achieve the freedom that she sought through the 'religious dimension' in a secular way? Can we achieve the 'intellectual
freedom' she rightly emphasises and adopt 'a habit of mind' allowing
us to make choices for ourselves without the domination and limit-
ing circumscriptions of the current System we inhabit—without 'the
devastating effects of ideological conditioning'? Even on the 'left' of
politics

---

2. Veronica Brady, 'Intellectual Belief and Freedom', in *Caught in the Draught*
   (Sydney: Angus and Robertson, 1994), 274. The essay is reprinted from *Meanjin*,
   50 (1991): 533–42; all page references are to the 1994 reprint.
3. Brady, 'Intellectual Belief and Freedom', 275.

a general sense prevails that all will be well if only we can be
more rational. Even women, who ought to know better, often
fail to see that the problem is systemic, that patriarchy's power
is essentially ideological . . .[4]

The problem then is one of having to find ways to escape the dominant ideology, or at least be in a position where challenging it is possible, and appeals to 'rationality' are of little use if the conception of
rationality in play is one that is already dominated by System, already
ideologically tainted.

However, I think that good philosophy can enable escape as well
as good theology can. The 'philosophical dimension' offers a secular
alternative to the religious dimension. But care is needed here. If the
philosophical dimension is underpinned, as it is typically taken to be,
by 'rationality' then we risk finding ourselves in the position of apply-
ing already-tainted standards of rationality in our attempts to think
our way past System and ideology.

The first hurdle is that much contemporary philosophy is reticent to abandon empiricist or positivist frameworks that, in essence,
restrict us precisely to that level of reality concerned with the observable world known to science—the philosopher's job, in this context,
is then to simply explore and justify such frameworks. Contemporary analytic philosophy (the domain in which I work) is dominated
by empiricism (the view that all knowledge is arrived at through the
physical senses) with its obvious emphasis on the observable. But
alternatives to empiricism exist—and have been championed by some
Australian philosophers (more on them soon). The second hurdle is
that much contemporary philosophy (both analytic and continental)
is reticent to abandon its anthropocentrism, especially in respect of
ethical ways of thinking and axiology more generally, thus restricting us in a crucial sense to precisely the 'human realm' that Veronica
sees a need to transcend. Again, one of Australia's greatest contribu-
tions to contemporary ethics is precisely a concerted attack on such
anthropocentrism. The religious dimension that Veronica appeals to
is both non-empiricist and non-anthropocentric and any secular philosophy we might appeal to must follow suit.

---

4. Brady, 'Intellectual Belief and Freedom', 276.

A useful way into this secular point of view comes from consideration of another point of criticism Veronica makes of 'rationality'. Speaking to Gail Jones in a 1997 interview, she comments:

> I think I see the enlightenment as collapsing before this particular [Australian] kind of environment and to me that is great news, theologically. Especially I think it is about time we finished with the cult of pure reason; true, there are many good things about the enlightenment, but this terror before what is different and what is other to me is the heart of racism, the heart of the imperial project. It is a project to control and to remake the world to your own image.[5]

'The enlightenment', and its conception of reason and rationality particularly, is seen as complicit in racism and fear of what is different; enlightenment reason encodes at its very heart a fear of the Other. Thus, from Veronica's theological perspective which demands compassion for those subjugated by this imperialism—both human Others (Aboriginal Australians) and non-human Others (the natural environment of this continent)—the collapse of 'the enlightenment', and its 'cult of pure reason', is to be welcomed.

However, it seems to me that one need not share her theological point of view to welcome such a collapse. The enlightenment 'reason' that she speaks of[6]—one that encodes racism (ethnic chauvinism, the view that *our* ethnic group is superior to any other), anthropocentrism (human chauvinism, the view that *our* species is superior to any other), androcentrism (male chauvinism, the view that the *male* gender is superior to any other) and (historically) class chauvinism (viewing the 'lower classes' as inferior)—has some strong secular, philosophical opponents. And two of the best are the Australian philosophers Richard and Val Routley—later known as Richard Sylvan and Val Plumwood.

---

5. Gail Jones, 'Veronica Brady', in *Journal of Australian Studies*, 21 (1997): 142.
6. Whether properly characterised as 'enlightenment reason' or not. I rather think not ('The Enlightenment' is too complex a period to exhibit a singular mode of reason), though I agree that it is a mode of thinking that is currently dominant in (at least) the West that, ironically, an ongoing process of enlightenment ought come to see as deeply flawed.

Sylvan and Plumwood were two of the twentieth century's most gifted, unorthodox, and original philosophers. They thought other philosophers were pretty much *all wrong about everything*. And their radical critique and reworking of logic, metaphysics, and ethics (especially environmental ethics—an academic sub-discipline they helped found) over thirty years, alongside a strong anarchist politics, resulted in a large body of work of startling originality.[7] Alan Lawson's characterisation of Veronica as showing 'a complete disregard for personal safety'—social as well as physical[8]—could equally well apply to them, with even a side-project like their extended critique of Australian forestry in the 1970s, *The Fight For the Forests*, bringing down the wrath of an entire industry upon them—a distinction afforded few philosophers. (Incidentally, it was this public policy critique that began their long friendship with Judith Wright and ultimately connected them to Veronica.)

Just as Veronica railed against ethnic injustice (especially gross injustices wrought against Aboriginal Australians), environmental injustice, class injustice and gender injustice, so too did Sylvan and Plumwood, but they appeal to the ultimate indefensibility of such injustice on *secular, philosophical* grounds. As with Veronica, a major driver for them was a rejection of the strong empiricism and imperialism that they saw pervading current ideology. And, like Veronica, they fought long and hard to overturn the deeply flawed and dangerous conception of reason and rationality that underpinned what they, too, saw as a grossly unjust world dominated by excessive instrumental rationality where too much was seen as a mere means to some cherished elite—male, upper class, white, European humans. But unlike Veronica, they used secular criticism to demand and describe a better way of thinking about and being in the world.

Veronica knew Val. They were connected through Judith Wright, as I said. Veronica was Wright's biographer and Val was Wright's friend and fellow environmental-activist and -theorist. Following Wright's death, they featured together in a wonderful Radio National tribute to her and, fellow travellers that they were, it was almost inevitable that they

---

7. For more on their remarkable lives and work see Dominic Hyde, in *Eco-Logical Lives: The Philosophical Lives of Richard Routley/Sylvan and Val Routley/Plumwood* (Cambridge: The White Horse Press, 2014).
8. Cited and elaborated on in Jones, 'Veronica Brady', 136.

should meet.[9] (It is interesting to note, I think, that alongside Veronica's religious expression of a way beyond impoverished 'reason' and Val's secular expression, we have Wright's poetic expression of what was essentially a similar goal—for she shared her husband Jack McKinney's horror at just what was done in the name of contemporary 'reason'.[10])

Plumwood's mature account of the flaws in this impoverished and impoverishing concept of reason and rationality is, perhaps, the most accessible of the various critiques offered by Sylvan and Plumwood. Plumwood, now most frequently described as an eco-feminist (and the foremost environmental philosopher of her generation), sought in later life to account for our current environmental crisis by showing that it was underpinned by a human chauvinism whose logic was the same as that which underpinned male chauvinism. In fact, ethnocentrism and class chauvinism were similarly linked. The ultimate source was a Hellenistic conception of reason as utterly opposed and superior to emotion—just note Plato's famous exhortation that reason must rule desire.

Grounded in the Pythagorean table of opposites, reason was separated from and contrasted with emotion. Reason was primary; emotion no more than 'unreason'. Thus a cult of reason was born (reaching its zenith in eighteenth and nineteenth century German Idealism). The Aristotelian conception of man as a 'rational animal' then links two further categories to this supposedly superior virtue—humans, and men in particular. Humans are superior to other animals (and, correspondingly, culture is superior to nature) since we exemplify this 'rationality'. And men are superior to women since rationality rules in men whereas women are ruled by their emotions. On this logic, then, women are 'closer to nature'. (The work of Australian feminist philosopher Genevieve Lloyd, *The Man of Reason*, was important to Plumwood's scholarly, philosophical analysis here.) The subjugation of nature and the subjugation of women are, in this way according to eco-feminism, linked. They both count as a kind of inferior Other. All of this, I think Veronica would agree with.

---

9. ABC Radio National, 'Rockpool by Judith Wright', *The Book Show*, (May 2008); interview with Michael Ackland, Veronica Brady and Val Plumwood at <http://www.abc.net.au/radionational/programs/bookshow/poetry-special-rockpool-by-judith-wright/3266950>. Accessed January 20 2016.
10. See his philosophical work, published by Wright: Jack McKinney, *The Challenge of Reason* (Brisbane: Mountain Press, 1950).

Now add to the mix (to cut a very long and complicated story short) the colonial idea of Aboriginal Australians as non-human, animal Others—most clearly evident in the false doctrine of *terra nullius*. As Veronica puts it:

> We assume that our ways are superior, inevitable and the only ones worthy of decent human beings. Locked within this ideology, most white Australians are unable to grant full humanity to Aborigines or their culture . . .[11]

And, similarly, the working classes are inferior. Thus we have arrived at a unified account of a 'logic of repression' according to which the subjugation of and associated presumed mastery over nature, women, indigenous peoples and the working classes proceeds by a defective kind of 'rationality' according to which they are all Other— all supposedly deficient in respect of the central virtue that places a very privileged class of people at the centre of the moral world—the virtue of reason as constructed in the Hellenistic foundations of the West. This is essentially Plumwood (and Sylvan's) environmental, post-colonial, feminist, and class critique. Correspondingly, Plumwood spoke of the 'logic of liberation', pursuing a kind of 'liberation philosophy' that is analogous in many ways to Veronica's 'liberation theology'—a logic that draws attention to and calls for a rejection of this flawed conception of rationality, the underlying 'cult of reason' that Veronica speaks of. So, I think, we can see why Veronica would welcome what she saw as the collapse of this 'cult'. But, importantly, the route mapped out here is a secular one.

Plumwood's position offers an alternative to current ideology, going on to describe an ethics of respect and care that elevates those subjugated by current ideology and condemns this ideology as immoral and indefensible. Her final work just prior to her death was devoted to developing a subtle and challenging form of animism, what she called 'materialist animism', aimed at redescribing the supposedly inanimate natural world of science and fact as one full of intention, goals, striving and value. What were considered mere objects are, in fact, subjects. This, too, was something Veronica would approve of. What Gail Jones has described as the 'animist inflection of her Catholicism' is evident in Veronica's essay 'Thinking as Feeling: Bill Neidjie's Story About Feeling'.

---

11. Brady, 'Intellectual Belief and Freedom', 279.

Our culture sees the external world as a source of information, something external to us to be exploited and developed for economic purposes or looked on for pleasure as a kind of panorama. But [in Neidjie's story] it is an aspect of self to be listened too, accepted in reverence . . .

> *That tree now, feeling . . .*
> *e blow . . .*
> *sit quiet you speaking . . .*
> *that tree now e speak . . .*
> *that wind e blow . . .*
> *e can listen . . .*

. . . The world . . . is a living experience, not something dead and inert . . . Where our attitude to the world . . . is antagonistic, this is agonistic. Self and world are intimately interrelated, living and moving together as lovers do . . . This cannot, I think, be dismissed as mere nature mysticism.[12]

Plumwood, too, was impressed by Neidjie's vision and went to Kakadu in 1983 to talk with him about it. Compare her later remarks after surviving her famous and horrendous attack by a saltwater crocodile there.

As the experience of being prey is eliminated from the face of the earth, along with it goes something it has to teach about the power and resistance of nature and the delusions of human arrogance.[13]

Nature, too, is agonistic; powerful and combative; 'living and moving' (as Veronica says) with an agency that sometimes delights us and sometimes is fearfully displayed.

This idea of the natural world as full of agency, full of animated subjects, presents us with a world imbued with value in the same way we see our subjective-selves as imbued. As subjects we matter, but so too does nature. This rejection of anthropocentrism is the final frontier. The Copernican revolution displaced us from the centre of the cosmic realm; the Darwinian revolution displaced us from the centre

12. Veronica Brady, 'Thinking as Feeling: Bill Neidjie's Story About Feeling', in *Caught in the Draught* (Sydney: Angus and Robertson, 1994), 46–7.
13. Val Plumwood, 'Human Vulnerability and the Experience of Being Prey', in *Quadrant*, March (1995): 34.

of the biological realm, and now, finally, we see ourselves displaced from the centre of the realm of agency and morality. Veronica's acceptance of this renders her theology immune to the environmental criticisms famously levelled at theists from the likes of Lynn White Jnr.[14] Not for her a natural world over which we have mastery by divine right. Her Franciscan theology is not culpable for 'our ecological crisis' that White saw as rooted in Christian ideas of dominion.[15]

With all this said, one might see the secular position outlined as just another form of rationalism, albeit a rationalism of new, enlightened type. But I think this misunderstands the full import of the foregoing analysis. If Plumwood's central, secular critique here is that the injustices that are wrought and misconceptions that are held (especially that of mastery over nature, women, and colonised peoples) themselves follow from an indefensible and objectionable conception of rationality—one that contrasts itself with emotion—then, amongst other consequences, another that follows is that reason and emotion are not discontinuous opposites. Each is, to some extent at least, a part of the other. Moreover, reason cannot, as has been the case, simply be assumed to be superior to emotion. Emotions must play a central a role in how we view the world alongside reason. In this sense then we can agree with Veronica that we need

> a redirection of thought away from the merely empirical and rational towards the intuitive, to 'realities at present unseen', which are beyond rational comprehension and control but can be argued about rationally.[16]

---

14. 'Christian attitudes toward man's relation to nature . . . are almost universally held not only by Christians and neo-Christians but also by those who fondly regard themselves as post-Christians. Despite Copernicus, all the cosmos rotates around our little globe. Despite Darwin, we are not, in our hearts, part of the natural process. We are superior to nature, contemptuous of it, willing to use it for our slightest whim.' (Lynn White Jnr, 'The Historical Roots of Our Ecological Crisis', in *Science*, 55 (1967): 1206–7).

15. White argued that St Francis of Assisi, 'the greatest spiritual revolutionary in Western history', provides 'an alternative Christian view' that led him to 'propose Francis as a patron saint for ecologists' (White, 'The Historical Roots of Our Ecological Crisis', 1207). His discussion here nicely illuminates the affinities between St Francis, Veronica and Plumwood (though Plumwood would want to distinguish her animism from Francis's 'panpsychism'). The influence of St Francis on Veronica is poignantly noted in Gail Jones' 'Eulogy for Sister Veronica Brady' (unpublished).

16. Brady, 'Intellectual Belief and Freedom', 278.

As Plumwood clearly emphasised towards the end of her life, appeals to emotion, the intuitive, are as important as appeals to reason. Or, to put the point differently, reason is sometimes not reason enough.[17] Her supplementation of argumentative philosophical work with increasingly narrative 'stories' describing what she wanted to say was ample evidence of this. In the end, we need literature, too, to effect the required changes. Veronica would have welcomed this too, I think.

Thus we see two thinkers, the arc of their respective intellectual enquiries converging—the secular and the religious. And in so doing, each comes to a position that marks them out as truly radical. Not for Plumwood the usual acceptance of the dogmas of philosophy; nor for Veronica the usual acceptance of the dogmas of religion. Both fearless, both independently-minded, and both passionate about justice—a passion that led each of them to push the very boundaries of their intellectual worlds. Veronica was a most curious theist indeed.

---

17. This claim must be stronger than the obvious psychological point that people often need more than reason to change their beliefs or be moved to action. (Those enamored of reason who *do* think reason is enough are often described as committing 'the philosopher's error'.) If Plumwood is right, it is the stronger claim that (sometimes, at least) emotions can function as grounds for belief every bit as 'rational' as reasons.

A Forum for a Theology in the World Vol 4 No 1&2/2017

God and Community and the Australian Catholic Nun

Paul Genoni

Sometime in 1975 I took my place in a lecture theatre at the University of Western Australia, as part of a unit on Australian Literature. Soon after the lecture commenced an elderly woman entered through a rear door and took the seat beside me. Perhaps typically, I soon became disenchanted with the lecture, gave up taking notes and commenced doodling. I drew, I scribbled, I made patterns, I jotted disparaging comments about the lecturer and other students. The elderly woman seemed interested in what I was doing. She smiled and apparently gave me encouragement, as a result of which I inclined the doodling in her direction so that she could fully appreciate my wit and skill. My scribblings became bolder, larger and increasingly designed to amuse my new friend. As the lecture finished she gave a final nod in my direction, rose and left the theatre.

The following week I occupied the same seat. Shortly before the lecture was due to commence my elderly new friend again entered through the rear door. Pleased to see her, I shuffled my chair along to make room. She ignored the offer, took the stairs down to the lectern, introduced herself as Veronica Brady, and commenced a lecture on Patrick White.

My embarrassment was profound. So this was THE Sister Veronica Brady, about whom I had heard so much, and of whom I already lived in trepidation on the basis of her formidable reputation for being formidable, and on my own experience of being easily intimidated by Catholic religious.

There are several things about that story that are, in retrospect, striking. First, the seemingly 'elderly' Veronica was only in her mid-40s at the time. Second, it seems almost inconceivable that the Veronica Brady I later came to know would indulge this type of misguided undergraduate posturing. Indeed I now believe that what I interpreted as encouragement was likely a means of quietly communicating that she had my measure.

With this lesson learnt I carefully avoided Veronica throughout my undergraduate years. Whereas others rushed to place their names on her over-subscribed tutorial lists, I just as eagerly went in other directions. When I planned, however, to return to study in the 1980s, with the intention of writing a thesis on Australian Catholic literature, she seemed to be the obvious supervisor. Gathering my courage on a November Tuesday morning, I knocked on her office door to broach the subject. Upon being admitted, I was instantly scolded for interrupting her while she was preparing a lecture. I might have quit and run immediately, except some poor young woman also interrupted at this point to ask Veronica how many tickets she would like in the day's Melbourne Cup sweep. The very curt and dismissive response to this polite question was sufficient to convince me that this nun had little in common with the Irish Catholics with whom I was familiar—clerics and lay persons alike—to whom Melbourne Cup Tuesday sat beside Ash Wednesday, Good Friday and Palm Sunday, as important dates on the liturgical calendar.

As it transpired Veronica was unavailable to supervise my research at that time. Either she was about to commence sabbatical leave, or was over-committed elsewhere—or perhaps she simply remembered our back row encounter from the previous decade and decided I wasn't worth the effort. Whatever the reason, I had to settle for far less capable supervision.

Exactly how different Veronica was from the suburban Catholic families, and the many priests, nuns and Christian Brothers who had pockmarked my childhood, I was soon to discover. In the absence of her supervision I decided to read what she might have written about Catholic literature and intellectual life in her book *A Crucible of Prophets*.[1] It had, after all, been written by a Catholic nun renowned for her scholarship on Australian literature, and surely she would have some insights to share about Catholic writing. What I found, however, was anything but a kindred spirit with a shared interest. Per-

---

1. Veronica Brady, *A Crucible of Prophets: Australians and the Question of God* (Sydney: Theological Explorations, 1981).

haps I should have been forewarned by the book's subtitle: *Australians and the Question of God*. There was a serious challenge in the phrasing of that sub-title—Veronica wasn't asking questions 'about God', a formulation with which I was familiar from my school catechisms; nor was she directing questions 'to God'—something few Catholics would assume to do. Rather she was tackling the big one, *the question of God*. It was not a question to which nuns were supposed to be in need of an answer.

Furthermore, I quickly realised I was in the presence of an unfamiliar, almost alien theology, when I encountered sentences and sentiments such as:

> The task of Australians . . . is to come to terms with their memories, their bodies and their environment and then to situate themselves as creatures within a mysterious, often painful but always worshipful cosmos.[2]

The Catholicism I knew did not consider us to be 'creatures'; did not refer to our earthly circumstances as part of a 'cosmos', and certainly did not favour us coming to terms with either our bodies or our environment. There was something almost neo-pagan, and certainly pantheistic about this view of the universe that was decidedly at odds with the Catholic worldview that steadfastly persisted in Australian suburbs and schools.

The argument presented in A *Crucible of Prophets* was also a revelation, suggesting that 'God', whoever or whatever that might be, is being created anew, and that how Australians conceive of God is determined by context, including our particular experience of place, time, local histories, languages, customs and traditions. Veronica found evidence for the revelation of this vernacular deity in a chronological discussion of key Australian writers who demonstrated an understanding of the mystery and sacredness of place, in particular Marcus Clarke, Rolf Boldrewood, Joseph Furphy, Patrick White, Randolph Stow, David Malouf and Christopher Koch. This pursuit of a localised and nationally expressive 'God' was a far cry from the reverence for the monolithic, albeit Trinitarian, deity at the centre of traditional Rome-centred Catholic devotion.

---

2. Brady, *A Crucible of Prophets*, 112.

Despite the apparently singular theology of *A Crucible of Prophets*, my ongoing research eventually led me to appreciate that, to a surprising extent, Veronica sat quite comfortably within her own generation of intellectually and spiritually ambitious Catholics. Indeed my reading became increasingly focused on the so-called 'cradle Catholics' of Veronica's generation. This included writers such as Morris West (b1916) Ruth Park (1923), Thea Astley, (1925), Criena Rohan (1928), Desmond O'Grady (1929), Peter Kenna (1930), Barry Oakley (1931), Christopher Koch (1932), Thomas Keneally (1935), Gerald Murnane (1939), Jack Hibberd (1940), Laurie Clancy (1942), and John Clanchy (1943), all of whom were born in the decade or so either side of Veronica (1929).

This was the generation that took the brunt of the Catholic Church's changing social and political circumstances, which were felt internationally but were particularly pronounced in Australia where the Church had been shaped by its long established position as a minority religion. In a country where the deep division between the dominant Anglo-Protestant group and the Irish-Catholics remained entrenched until well into the twentieth century, Catholicism had developed as a remarkably tribal experience with its identity wedded to a deep sense of community and a conservative, priest-focused theology.

Inevitably, however, the ground beneath traditional Australian Catholicism began to shift. After the Second War various cracks appeared in the solidarity of the Australian Church, with milestones being the mid-50s split within the Labor Party that fractured the powerful Catholic bloc and led to the creation of the Democratic Labor Party dominated by disaffected conservative Catholics, and the liberalising Second Vatican Council of the early 1960s, which further exacerbated divisions between the Church's progressives and conservatives.

At a personal level many Catholics, including Veronica Brady, were to benefit from the incremental modernisation of the Church that occurred during this period. One crucial change was the increased access to universities for the post-war generation. While the Church had long cautioned young Catholics that a university education was unsuited to their moral and intellectual development, Brady, along with Astley, O'Grady, Oakley, Koch, Hibberd, Murnane, Clancy and Clanchy all went to University in the post war years. In almost every case they were the first in their family to do so—as indeed was Veronica.

As it transpired the conservative Church hierarchy had cause for concern, because as numerous Catholics who entered the universities in the 1940s and 50s have attested, the experience had a remarkably liberating impact which tested the faith of developing intellects. Poet Josie Arnold, who commenced at Melbourne University in the 1950s, was one who recalled the sudden expansion of intellectual possibilities:

> This was capital L-Life. This was a magic castle of rooms labelled wonderfully: Philosophy, Classics, Modern Languages, Psychology . . . It was foreign to everything in my everyday life . . . lecturers had a briskness and appeal to reason that was a healthy antidote to the religiosity that had dominated my secondary schooling . . . I had not lost my faith as Sister Matthew had so dolefully predicted, but I skilfully remodelled it to fit my developing personality. Although I still harboured a strong inner desire for meditation, it was evident that my vocation to be a nun had been a product of my school environment that wilted in a world that was no more 'real' than my school, but very different.[3]

The Church responded by encouraging university based Catholic communities in the form of Newman and Campion Societies, as a way of supporting traditional Catholic values. Most Catholic students, including the young Veronica at Melbourne University, joined these groups, very likely seeking continuity with their own parish communal life, but finding instead that they served a contrary purpose by giving a platform to intellectually adventurous colleagues wanting to challenge traditional Church authority and dogma. Indeed the leaders within these societies saw to it that they encouraged the very liberal, humanistic thinking that so concerned the church and challenged its authority. Priest and critic Edmund Campion later recalled that, 'From our involvement in the Newman Society at the University we learnt that *we*, as much as the bishops and priests, were the Church'.[4]

---

3. Josie Arnold, *Mother Superior, Woman Inferior* (Blackburn: Dove, 1985), 110–12.
4. Edmund Campion, *Rockchoppers: Growing Up Catholic in Australia* (Ringwood: Penguin, 1982), 165.

Campion was also amongst many students who found the university societies became a gateway to Catholic literature from more liberal traditions that were open to more individualised and spiritually adventurous apprehensions of God and that were therefore a further challenge to the traditional link between Rome and home. By her own account Veronica started reading the work of French Catholics such as Georges Bernanos and Francois Mauriac—writers who provided a signal to look beyond the Irish Catholic community in favour of a more personal spirituality and conception of God—Christopher Koch is among those who have recalled approvingly of Bernanos' condemnation of the tedium of parish life.[5]

The result was that Veronica Brady found herself part of a generation of Catholics coming of age in a community and religion that were suddenly vulnerable to a secularising modernity. In the words of Catholic social commentator Karl Schmude:

> One might say they were born between two religious cultures, one dying, the other struggling to be born, and they received their formation in the matrix of a Church on the threshold of transformation. They were brought up in a way of life ceasing to believe in itself.[6]

This eventually became the generation that churned out the 'lapsed Catholic' novels and plays that became a cliché of the 1960s and 70s. James Joyce had written the prototype as early as 1916 with *Portrait of the Artist as a Young Man*. One need hardly spend time arguing for the influence of Joyce, or *The Portrait of the Artist*, on twentieth century literature. The novel tapped into a theme as old and rich as language, that of the clash between generations and the need for the young to find their own identity and system of belief, but it did so in a manner that seemed entirely modern and that eventually resonated with several generations of intellectually adventurous young Catholics in mid-century Australia. As Christopher Koch has written:

---

5. CJ Koch, *Crossing the Gap* (London: Hogarth, 1987), 139–41.
6. Karl Schmude, 'The Changing Accent of Catholic Literature', in *Quadrant* (January–February 1984): 56.

> I read ... Joyce's *Portrait of the Artist as a Young Man* at sixteen,
> and [it] had a profound effect on me ... I found that a Dublin
> Catholic boyhood in no way differed from a Hobart one at
> St Virgil's college in the 1940's, with its Irish brothers. Father
> Doolan with his pandy bat was no stranger to me, except
> that at St Virgil's he wielded a strap, known affectionately as
> Doctor Black.[7]

Or, as the eponymous hero of Desmond O'Grady's *Deschooling Kevin Carew* put it, 'Stephen Hero and A Portrait were the only novels which spoke to his condition.'[8]

Following Morris West's *Moon in My Pocket* from 1945, (published under the pseudonym Julian Morris in order to safeguard the author's anonymity), the heavily Joycean genre of the Irish-Catholic *künstler-roman* (artist-novel) was established in Australia.[9] To the Irish-Catholics, the role given to the artist as being that of someone dedicated to the task of personal expression, in whatever form, deftly symbolised their need for personal expression that at once ostracised them from both their native community and its conservative religion. Novels by Australian Catholics that adhere to the form of the *künstlerroman* include Christopher Koch's *The Boys in the Island* (1958)[10] and *The Doubleman* (1985); Desmond O'Grady's, *Deschooling Kevin Carew* (1974); Barry Oakley's *A Wild Ass of a Man* (1967); Laurie Clancy's *A*

---

7. Christopher Koch, 'Growing up and the Getting of Wisdom', in *A Common Wealth of Words*, edited by Maureen Freer and Ken Goodwin (Spring Hill: Boolarong, 1982), 73–4.
8. Desmond O'Grady, *Deschooling Kevin Carew* (Melbourne: Wren, 1974), 54. 'Stephen Hero' is a reference to a posthumously published novel by Joyce of that name that has many thematic similarities to *A Portrait of the Artist as a Young Man*.
9. Julian Morris, *Moon in My Pocket* (Sydney: Australasian Publishing, 1945).
10. The most memorable figure in *Boys in the Island* is Shane Noonan; a young man of artistic temperament and Jesuit education, who is fighting attempts to have him abandon his dreams of writing poetry and take up with the family business. Unable to reconcile his own needs with the demands of his family, he eventually commits suicide by throwing himself beneath a St Kilda train. Koch has written that the character of Shane Noonan was based on young Tasmanian poet Tony Wren, noting that 'only an Irish Catholic could understand the madness of the situation which drove Tony to his death, and robbed us of a remarkable poet. He was literally *not allowed* to be a poet' (Christopher Koch, 'CJ Koch comments', in *Quadrant* [December 1980]: 40–1).

Collapsible Man (1975); David Parker's *Building on Sand* (1988); John Hanrahan's *O Excellent Virgin* (1990); and much of the fiction of Gerald Murnane. Australian Catholic women were a little later coming to the genre, but examples include Jennifer Dabbs' *Beyond Redemption* (1987); Penelope Rowe's *Tiger Country* (1990), and Davida Allen's *Close to the Bone* (1991).[11]

These novels ranged from very good to indifferent, but they followed a broadly similar theme. Devout young Catholic goes to university and discovers thinking contrary to his/her childhood religion; discovers his/her artistic self; discovers a newer and funkier version of God; discovers they no longer fit with Church/family/community; discovers their life is now pretty much the hellish, immoral mess they were warned it would become; discovers there is no turning back as s/he blunders onwards in search of their personal forms of artistic expression and a new community.

The existential trap, however, was that while they might have rejected their communal religion, they were nonetheless predisposed by their upbringing to continue believing in the spiritual and the miraculous. Thea Astley stated that 'I'm no longer a practicing Catholic, but I do believe in God'[12]; Christopher Koch that 'I believe firmly in mysteries as a result of my Catholic training';[13] and Thomas Keneally that, 'I still believe in the Other or the Absolute. I believe in that as naturally as believing in anything.'[14] As a result of this unshakeable belief in some form of otherworldly influence, the literary characters they created find themselves bereft of both their inherited community and its God, but unable to forge suitable replacements. By novel's end they have become the stock figure of the estranged, tormented and guilt-ridden lapsed Catholic. As Joyce had brilliantly demonstrated, the tale of the gifted outcast is particularly

---

11. The Catholic outsider is not unique to fiction. One of the best known examples in Australian literature can be found in the character of hermit and 'Old Xaverian' Monk O'Neill in Jack Hibberd's play *A Stretch of the Imagination* (Sydney: Currency, 1973).

12. Thea Astley, in Jennifer Ellison, *Rooms of Their Own* (Ringwood: Penguin, 1986), 66.

13. Christopher Koch, in 'Christopher Koch in conversation with Michael Hulse', in *Quadrant* (June1985): 25.

14. Thomas Keneally', in Terry Lane, *As the Twig is Bent* (Melbourne: Dove, 1979), 130.

poignant when coupled with the clash of sensibilities that occurs as the Catholic artist struggles to achieve his vision and claim his freedom from the tribe.

In its classic form, the hero of the *künstlerroman* typically grows from youth to maturity, from innocence and even ignorance into a mature artistic consciousness. For the young artist, this latter state is usually achieved only after coming to terms with, or escaping from, the restrictive boundaries of a communal situation that is unsupportive of their creative ambition. As Maurice Beebe has written, the hero must rid him/herself of:

> the domestic, social, and religious demands imposed upon him by his environment. Narrative development in the typical artist-novel requires that the hero test and reject the claims of love and life, of God, home and country, until nothing is left but his true self and his consecration as artist.[15]

Inevitably the artist-hero's sensitivity and individuality mean that their artistic ambitions lead them to values which are antithetical to those of their native community, but they remain at least attracted to that community by the recognition that they can truly belong to no other. The artist therefore becomes both representative and outsider.

In this critical regard the Australian-Catholic novels fail to meet the expectations of a *künstlerroman*, and also fail to emulate *A Portrait of the Artist as a Young Man*, in that the hero is ultimately unable to achieve the realisation of his or her artistic destiny. Unlike Stephen Daedalus who is possessed of a real vision for his creative gift and how it may serve to reveal something of the true nature of God, for many of the heroes of these Australian novels their 'creativity' is little more than a means of distancing themselves from both their community and God. Their artistic expression, in whatever form it may take, lacks the vision and the clarity required to assist them in achieving a real spiritual autonomy. They find that their desire for release and escape, and their attempt to realise their art, is frustrated, and for quite similar reasons—try as they might to forge something new and individual, in the end they are irredeemably constrained by the conservative community to which they were born. These novels

---

15. Maurice Beebe, *Ivory Towers and Sacred Founts: The Artist as Hero in Fiction from Goethe to Joyce* (New York: New York University Press, 1964), 6.

therefore adhere to the generalities of Joyce's novel, but they are ultimately unable to render its essential spirit of growth and discovery.

For example Muldoon, the hero of Barry Oakley's *A Wild Ass of a Man*, is almost frantic in his attempt to create a life apart from native his Irish-Catholic community. The novel's title is culled from a passage in Genesis that serves as an epigram to the novel, and establishes the theme of the outsider;

> He shall be a wild ass of a man,
> his hand against everyone,
> And everyone's hand against him;
> he shall dwell apart, opposing all his kinsmen.

Muldoon starts life firmly amongst his kinsmen, in an Irish Catholic family from a poor inner city parish. He is possessed, however, of a desire to escape. It is a desire born in part of the poverty of his community and their status as 'outsiders', but more urgently by 'the old, the atavistic, the pristine urge to be God'.[16] Muldoon doesn't quite know what to make of this urge. He briefly attends university; meddles with the Newman Society; forsakes his religion; develops a great appetite for life and experience; has a series of unsatisfactory personal relationships; attempts several artistic careers; and eventually finds himself desperate, alone and unfulfilled. He is as he says, one of those 'who never quite know what they *want*, all they know is that this isn't it'.[17]

Muldoon's expiation is a brief concluding chapter, in which he accepts his all too obvious limitations. He is back within the bosom of his community, in fact within a religious community, 'as a lay brother of the Lord'. He is now cloistered and submissive, no longer pushing at the bonds of his religion, but content to accept the authority of the Church and its community as the only satisfactory method of honouring the distant and largely unknowable God.

Thematically Laurie Clancy's novel *A Collapsible Man* (1975), has much in common with *A Wild Ass of a Man*, while also pointing the way to the an alternative fate, that of the artist who uses his art to force a wedge between himself and his community, and who resolutely dissipates both himself and his art in the struggle to maintain the separation. The central character on this occasion is Paul O'Donahue,

---

16. Barry Oakley, *A Wild Ass of a Man* (Ringwood: Penguin,1970), 4.
17. Oakley, *A Wild Ass of a Man*, 45.

who tells the reader of his upbringing that, 'In almost every sense it was the classic pattern of Irish Catholics in Australia'[18] The details of a Christian Brothers schooling, the impact of time spent at university, and ineptitude in personal and sexual relations are repeated. O'Donahue's response is to assiduously cultivate his role as the outsider who refuses to conform to the expectations of the native religion and community, and who uses his literary ambitions in order to distance himself from them.

As O'Donahue gradually abandons all attachments to his community, his decline is unrelieved. He takes to alcohol, revels in self-loathing, drives away those who may be able to help him, dissipates his scant literary talents, and is eventually admitted to a home for the mentally disturbed. O'Donahue realises the nature of his mistakes and missed opportunities, but he remains unrepentant. He has chosen his path in life, and even at the novel's conclusion he is still looking to take his search for random experience even further.

The fates that befall Muldoon and O'Donahue are typical of those found in other examples of the Australian Catholic *künstlerroman*. Each young artist, in the manner of Stephen Daedalus, attempts in his or her manner to leave the community and to pursue their own 'God', but each fails to meet the challenge on which they have embarked. They may reject traditional Irish-Catholicism with its austere God, entrenched dogma and arcane forms of worship, but they have no other theological or intellectual traditions to which they can turn. Their need for independence remains unfocussed at best and destructively solipsistic at worst. Ultimately they are either drawn back into the bosom of the community, as is Muldoon, or they choose a path to isolation and spiritual debilitation, as does O'Donahue. Either way, they surrender their art in the process.

Veronica Brady may not have gone on to a notable career as a creative writer—her sometimes fine poetry not withstanding—but as with other Catholic intellectuals of her generation she too suffered the pangs of personal decision making as she found her spiritual and communal allegiances challenged. Not surprisingly, both God and community had influenced Veronica's decision to become a Loreto nun. Whenever she spoke of this decision in later life she unfailingly mentioned the exposure to the sacred that she had felt

---

18. Laurie Clancy, *A Collapsible Man* (Fitzroy: Outback, 1979), 24.

had been imparted through her personal experience of the numinous at a young age, while also noting the sense of belonging the Church gave her, both through her participation in Church ritual and also the happy and cooperative communities that she observed within convents.

Veronica was not alone amongst her generation of intellectually-inclined and university educated Catholics in finding appeal in the ordained life. West, Keneally, Murnane, and Windsor all spent time in seminaries, although none proceeded to final vows. Whereas these men left after finding that the institutional Church could not accommodate the various intellectual freedoms they sought, Veronica spent her adult life in the Loreto order, despite being similarly disenchanted with aspects of the traditional Church. It was undoubtedly a difficult choice for individuals to leave the Church whether or not they had attempted an ordained life. As Thomas Keneally noted:

> It's a shock to think that you're the first member of your family since the dark ages who hasn't been a Catholic. It's a bit awesome. You wonder if you are doing the dirt on all the others.[19]

It also cannot have been straightforward for Veronica to remain within a religious order as she became disenchanted with many aspects of Church leadership and doctrine. She was fortunate in that the Loreto order provided more freedom of movement and employment than was the case in other orders, and like Josie Arnold, she seems to have accommodated her faith according to her developing personality—for which we can read her evolving intellectual life with its focus on social justice, and a more liberal and inclusive conception of God. When questioned about her religious beliefs Veronica eventually took to describing herself as an 'unbelieving believer'. Now that is a slippery phrase, but it certainly implies a conscious distancing from the source of her faith, and it seems that she chose her words as a way of signalling that while she continued to believe in a Christian God, that it was also necessarily unlike the God that continued to prevail in many Australian Catholic homes, schools and communities.

As Veronica's conception of God evolved, so too did her vision of community. She eventually found some communal aspects of the

---

19. Keneally, *As the Twig is Bent,* 129.

Church, and indeed of the convent, frustrating and restricting, and as a result of both her growing identification with left-wing, liberal politics and a certain fastidiousness in her personal habits she eventually spent periods living outside the Loreto community. Her sense of community had, however, expanded beyond the confines of the convent, or the order, or the Church, to the point where she was very comfortable generalising about the spiritual and sacred lives of 'Australians', as she had done in *A Crucible of Prophets*. If the God she came to worship was one that reflected the particularities of her own time and place, then the community with which she wanted to share that God was one built on a vision of the 'nation', of all Australians. Whereas reference to a nation-wide identity might serve other literary critics as a sort of rhetorical sleight of hand—a way of appealing to the authority of a subjectivity at once independent of, and more inclusive, than their own—I believe that for Veronica it was a genuine and deep part of both her evolving conception of God and her commitment to an inclusive social justice. These two things were, I believe, intimately aligned for Veronica. As former Catholic schoolboy Kerry O'Brien commented when interviewed by Julia Zemiro for ABC television's *Home Delivery*, 'For a thinking Catholic, the brand is social conscience'.

It is arguable that Veronica Brady succeeded, where so many other Irish-Catholics intellectuals of her generation failed, in fulfilling the ambition of using her art to forge a new notion of both God and community. By her 'art' I refer to her important literary scholarship, her vision of social inclusion and environmental responsibility, and her power as an advocate. As a result she was demonstrably able to create a new and individual path, one that intimately connected her art to the way she thought, lived and expressed herself, but which also resulted in her also continuing to call upon the structure and nourishment provided by her inherited God and community.

I would like to note that one interest I shared with Veronica was the Camino de Santiago, Europe's greatest Christian pilgrimage with a history stretching back over a millennium, and which has undergone a remarkable revitalisation in recent decades. Despite having its roots in traditional Catholic dogma and worship (in this case of the supposed relics of the apostle James interred in the Spanish city of Santiago de Compostela), the contemporary Camino is nonetheless a secular pathway where pilgrims come in search of many forms of revelation and redemption while bonding with an international cast of fellow seekers. The Camino has become yet another place where God and community rub shoulders, sometimes in harmony, and sometimes in tension.

My interest in the Camino is a scholarly curiosity about contemporary literary representations of the pilgrimage, particularly those written by Australians.[20] Veronica, however, was more hands on—or perhaps feet on—in that in 1999 she walked much of the 800 kilometres of the stretch of the Camino that leads from the Franco-Spanish border to Santiago de Compostela. I am grateful to Kath Jordan's biography for what I know of Veronica's experience on the Camino, because she undertook the journey with Veronica and wrote about it in some detail.[21] Veronica also left her own, more sketchy account in an interview recorded at the Perth Writer's Festival the year following her pilgrimage. Earlier in her life Veronica had written that 'We are a pilgrim people', and in talking about the Camino she of course demonstrated a deep appreciation of the symbolic and literary value of pilgrimage—as she observed 'it's a metaphor for who we all are: we're all people on the way, and going somewhere'.[22] In those few words she expresses again that her life journey involved a case of community—'we're all people on the way'—and a spiritual quest—'we are all going somewhere'. As Jordan reported, however, although acknowledging the importance of community on the Camino, Veronica shunned the demands of shared living in the dormitory style *refugios* that are the choice of those seeking an 'authentic' pilgrim experience, preferring her solitary comforts to the more communal experience. She also rejected the journey's purported spiritual destination, reporting that the city of Santiago is 'repulsive in the extreme'.[23] As was so often the case, Veronica trod her own path, in her own way.

As Veronica noted when recounting her pilgrimage, she had also, in some senses, 'cheated' on the Camino. Daunted by the Pyr-

---

20. Paul Genoni, 'The Australian way: transnational flows and the 21th century Camino', in *The Camino de Santiago in the 21s Century*, edited by Samuel Sánchez y Sánchez and Annie Hesp (New York: Routledge, 2016), 172–93.

21. Kath Jordan, *Larrikin Angel: A Biography of Veronica Brady* (South Fremantle: Round House, 2009), 245–55.

22. ABC, 'Spanish pilgrimage', *Arts Talk*, Saturday 23 April 2011, available at: http://www.abc.net.au/radionational/programs/replay/spanish-pilgrimage/3005876

23. ABC.

enees and other inhospitable sections of the walk she occasionally used taxis or buses, to carry either herself or her backpack, a practice frowned upon by those seeking to identify with the experience of authentic mediaeval pilgrimage. While her choice was understandable for someone in her 70th year, it somewhat undermined the metaphorical value of the pilgrimage when applied to her own life journey—Veronica Brady was certainly not given to shortcuts, not one to avoid the hard parts, and not one who expected anyone else to carry her load. Indeed Veronica was devoted to the journey—I think she learnt early in life that she was the sort of pilgrim who preferred travelling to arrival.

In addition to recalling my first encounter with Veronica, I also remember the last. Over three decades after that first 'meeting' I fell into conversation with her at a book launch, and once again I also fell into error. This time I made the mistake of enquiring after her retirement. She immediately rankled, announcing that she didn't, and never would, consider herself retired. 'There are always ideas' she declared, 'ideas are all that matter'.

This unending quest for, and testing of, ideas is vividly reflected in how Veronica Brady lived her life, and goes some way to explaining why she has left a deep legacy with her activism and her writing. As a pilgrim she forged her own path, prepared to travel in company, but resolved, if necessary, to move on alone. Faced with the possibility of being alone, she was prepared to encompass a nation. Embarking on a journey, she was happy to be unsure of her destination. In search of a new God and a new community she refused to be confined by anyone else's conception of what it meant to be a nun. She was prepared to ask the question of God, with the expectation that there was no answer. Thinkers and writers of her type provide the only texts we should trust.

'A Symbolic Opening Towards the Future': Veronica Brady on *Mabo*

Kieran Dolin

On one of her many visits to the Arts building at UWA after retiring, Veronica asked me if I had read John D Caputo's *The Prayers and Tears of Jacques Derrida*.[1] I had not, but neither was I surprised that Veronica was abreast of new developments in critical theory, and recommending her discoveries to others. One of the hallmarks of Veronica's lectures was the way that she placed literary texts into dialogue with philosophy and history, connecting the plots, characters and symbols of literature with broader cultural concerns. She radiated a sense of intellectual energy, of reading as passionate discovery, of literature as a search for complex and important truths. I would often head straight to the library after these lectures, to follow up the references in her handouts while the connections were still fresh in the mind. Veronica's writings exhibit similar methods and commitments, and through the rhythm of her exposition preserve traces of her unique critical voice. Not only does she cite passages from diverse sources to open up the significance of literary texts, but she also brings the insights of fiction and poetry to the analysis of ethical and social issues. In this way, the literary imagination becomes a resource in the search for wisdom. Yet as her recommendation of Caputo's book shows, in Veronica's hands this search comports with a deeply critical spirit. *The Prayers and Tears of Jacques Derrida* puts deconstruction in dialogue with theology. In the same way, Veronica put literature and literary criticism in dialogue with theology, pursuing what Nicholas Boyle calls 'literature as a "site" of theology' and

---

1. John D Caputo, *The Prayers and Tears of Jacques Derrida: Religion without Religion* (Bloomington: Indiana University Press, 1997).

opening the latter to potential insights from other disciplines or bodies of knowledge such as deconstruction or post-colonialism.[2] In this paper I shall be examining Veronica's collection, *Caught in the Draught*, particularly its focus on Aboriginal justice through the lens of a theological approach to Australian literature.[3]

Boyle draws the phrase, 'literature as the "site" of theology' from a 1969 article of that name by Marie-Dominique Chenu OP, in which Chenu hoped that an understanding of literature, especially the Bible, would enable theology to 'live in symbiosis with all human culture.'[4] While this vision of the inter-animation of faith and culture was central to the renewal of the Catholic Church promoted by the Second Vatican Council, and to Veronica's life and critical practice, the universalism of this formulation raises questions when viewed in a post-colonial light, as seems necessary in Australia today. For Veronica, theology was to be broadly conceived, 'the attempt to understand the meaning of God and of our human and historical existence,' as she put it in her article on the Indian Catholic poet Eunice De Souza.[5] Her approach also draws on the critical tradition of Nietzsche and Kierkegaard, as is well known:

> There is always a tension between God as God and any words we use about him, or any institutions which claim to represent him. This is especially true of theology which by definition involves a kind of closure, since it involves thinking about God, the totally Other, in terms which are culturally conditioned.[6]

In her detailed and appreciative account of Eunice De Souza, Veronica shows the poet's engagement with Hindu as well as Catholic traditions, and her resultant ability to 'see and dramatise the connection

---

2. See Nicholas Boyle, *Sacred and Secular Scriptures: A Catholic Approach to Literature* (London: Darton, Longman and Todd, 2004), chapter 1.
3. Veronica Brady, *Caught in the Draught: On Contemporary Australian Culture and Society* (Sydney: Angus and Robertson, 1994).
4. Boyle, *Sacred and Secular Scriptures*, 4, quoting Chenu, 'La littérature comme "lieu" de la théologie.' The translation from Chenu is by Boyle.
5. This description of the scope of theology, one of many in Veronica Brady's writings, is taken from 'One Long Cry in the Dark'?: The Poetry of Eunice De Souza', in *Literature and Theology* 5/1 (1991): 122.
6. Brady, 'Cry in the Dark,' 108.

between the institutional church and Western cultural imperialism.[7] This article in the leading journal, *Literature and Theology*, usefully registers the scope and orientation of Veronica's work in this interdisciplinary field, her location of faith in history:

> a theological response is . . . one which seeks to be attentive to the resonances within the words of the primal Word, and, situating the poems within history, [reads] them also in the context of the play and process of that Word within history.[8]

In 'The Articulation of Silence' Veronica noted that the theological was 'a forbidden category' in contemporary Australian humanities debates, and defended it as a broad discourse of ultimate values:

> the word, as Kevin Hart points out, 'pertains . . . to the use of any vocabulary in which meaning or being is said to be wholly resolved by reference to an origin, end, centre or ground.' Nor does talk of 'centres' or 'grounds' offend against the insights of contemporary theory . . . The ground at issue here is that of language itself.[9]

Having had the formative experience of studying and teaching Australian literature with Veronica, I want in this paper to revisit one of her major interests, that of understanding and achieving proper relations between Aboriginal and non-Aboriginal people in Australia. This was foregrounded in the syllabus of the time, which began with *Coonardoo* and *Capricornia*, and included Kevin Gilbert's *Living Black* as well as Judith Wright, Patrick White and Randolph Stow. It is also the subject of her extended study, *Can These Bones Live?*, and also of her collection of papers, *Caught in the Draught*.[10] The first paper in the latter book, 'Mabo: A Question of Space,' is an examination of the backlash against the 1992 High Court judgment in *Mabo*

---

7. Brady, 'Cry in the Dark', 108.
8. Brady, 'Cry in the Dark', 101.
9. Veronica Brady, 'The Articulation of Silence: Finding What has been Buried Alive,' in *Caught in the Draught*, 91. This text was originally delivered as the Dorothy Green Lecture to the annual conference of the Association for the Study of Australian Literature in 1992.
10. Veronica Brady, *Can These Bones Live?* (Leichhardt: Federation Press, 1996). Originally delivered as the New College Lectures, University of New South Wales, 1988.

v Queensland that recognised native title as part of the common law in Australia.[11] This primacy reflects the cultural importance of the decision, and its potential contribution to what Veronica regarded as possibly 'the crucial problem' facing the nation, namely, 'our relations with Aboriginal people and their culture, and with the long and brutal history of our invasion and occupation of this country'.[12]

Mabo was immediately perceived as a potentially transformative decision of national importance due to its overturning of the founding assumption of colonial law, that Australia was a *terra nullius*—a land without owners, a land without a settled law or government—or, in the words of Blackstone, 'desert and uncultivated' land.[13] As a legal proceeding that brought the law into accord with modern understandings of Aboriginal social organisation, *Mabo* exemplified a key feature of the genre of the 'case' as described by James Chandler:

> the case is not merely an instantiation of a general scheme or normative system; nor is it just the form in which that instantiation occurs. Rather it is the occurrence of an anomaly for such a system or scheme. In the case we see the posing of a problem for the framework in respect to which the object or event is represented.[14]

The *Mabo* case placed evidence of the reality of Indigenous communities' ownership of their traditional lands before the court, thus forcing it to confront the fundamental legal fiction of *terra nullius*. Not surprisingly, in resolving this 'anomaly' by recognising native title while taking care to preserve all other aspects of Australian law, the decision elicited strong reactions, both positive and negative. Conservative politicians and scholars protested at the overruling of a long-standing precedent, and feared its effects on the regime of property law in Australia.[15] Academics from a socio-legal studies or

---

11. Brady, *Caught in the Draught*, 13–29.
12. Veronica Brady, 'Intellectual Belief and Freedom,' in *Caught in the Draught*, 278–9.
13. Sir William Blackstone, *Commentaries on the Laws of England*, 1765–9 (London: Dawsons of Pall Mall, 1966), I. 104.
14. James K Chandler, *England in 1819: The Politics of Literary Culture and the Case of Romantic Historicism* (Chicago: University of Chicago Press, 1998), 207–8.
15. See for example, Geoffrey Partington, 'Thoughts on Terra Nullius,' Proceedings of the Nineteenth Conference of the Sir Samuel Griffith Society, Melbourne, 2007. http://www.samuelgriffith.org.au/papers/html/volume19/v19chap11.html

legal humanities background critiqued the reasoning and the limitations of the decision.[16] Property law academics tended to see it as an organic development of the law and one that had long been adopted in comparable countries.

Beyond the legal effects, the wider implications of the decision for a more truly inclusive national community and for a postcolonial reconstituting of its legal basis were also quickly discerned. A number of public intellectuals noted the High Court's reliance on modern historical and anthropological research, and saw the decision as entailing a new narrative for the Australian nation, and calling forth the hope for a new moral community.[17] The then Prime Minister, Paul Keating, attempted to mobilise public support for the development of such a vision, tying native title and racial justice into a political programme for an Australian republic. Analysing Keating's rhetoric around this 'historic decision', Bain Attwood identified a desire to 'contain' or 'subsume' the emerging awareness of Aboriginal rights within a discourse of national unity.[18] Attwood recognises the historical significance of the case—his edited collection is called *In the Age of Mabo*—but he regards the decision as 'part of a *process* rather than . . . a mere *event*.'[19] That is, while there was evidence the judgment was 'supported by a broad cross-section of Australian settler opinion,' it did not represent a definitive break with the ideology of the colonialist past.[20] John Morton, in a survey of popular culture that formed his contribution to Attwood's volume, saw signs of new tropes and figures that suggested a refashioning of national genealogies in the

---

16. Penelope Pether, 'Principles or Skeletons? *Mabo* and the Discursive Constitution of Australia', in *Law/Text/Culture,* 4 (1998): 115–45.

17. See for example, Tim Rowse, *After Mabo: Interpreting Indigenous Traditions* (Melbourne: Melbourne University Press, 1993); Nonie Sharp, *No Ordinary Judgment: Mabo, the Murray Islanders' Land Case* (Canberra: Aboriginal Studies Press, 1996); Felicity Collins and Therese Davis, *Australian Cinema after Mabo* (Melbourne: Cambridge University Press, 2004).

18. Bain Attwood, editor *In the Age of Mabo* (North Sydney: Allen and Unwin, 1996), xxxv.

19. Attwood, *Age of Mabo*, 150, n 154. Italics in original. Attwood argues that a number of his co-contributors share this view.

20. Attwood, *Age of Mabo*, xxxv.

field of popular entertainment as well as history, but also observed that this process was 'highly contested'.[21]

Many Indigenous people were elated by the decision. Larissa Behrendt, a lawyer and writer and member of the Kamilaroi and Eualeyai people, reflected ten years after the judgment that

> the elation about the overturning of the doctrine of terra nullius was deserved, and . . . the case can be seen as an important legal, symbolic and psychological turning point. In that way the *Mabo* case remains a solid reminder that historical wrongs can be righted.[22]

Nevertheless, Behrendt argued, the old ideologies survived in the form of a 'psychological *terra nullius*' through which a romanticised view of settler history led to attempts to limit or extinguish Indigenous property rights.[23] Mick Dodson highlighted the limitations and deficiencies of *Mabo* in a scathing assessment soon after the decision:

> The *Mabo* decision does not recognise equality of rights or equality of entitlement: it recognises the legal validity of Aboriginal title until the white man wants that land . . . For the vast majority of Indigenous Australians the *Mabo* decision is a belated act of sterile symbolism. It will not return the country of our ancestors, nor will it result in compensation for its loss.

While Dodson was rightly more interested in the practical effects of the decision, rather than any symbolic meanings, Veronica's paper, 'Mabo: A Question of Space', uses symbolism as a means of understanding its reception. Her point of departure is the negative reaction to the *Mabo* decision, which was particularly virulent in Western Australia, and which gathered strength nationally with the defeat of Keating and the election of John Howard as Prime Minister in 1996. Veronica sets herself to understand the causes of the 'storm of protest'

---

21. John Morton, 'Aboriginality, Mabo and the Republic: Indigenising Australia,' in Attwood, *Age of Mabo*, 119.
22. Larissa Behrendt, 'Mabo Ten Years On', paper delivered to forum on 'The Legacy of Mabo', Australian National University, 6 June 2002, 1.
23. Behrendt, 'Mabo Ten Years On', 5.

and the disturbing 'residue of anti-Aboriginal, even racist, feeling' that accompanied it. She correctly discerned that the intensity of this response reflected what Mark Davis has called a 'symbolic politics of race', and that it could most effectively be opposed by analysing the symbols and myths in which Australian understandings of race were encoded.[24] Noting that processes of 'exclusion and circumscription' are part of all assertions of national identity, and strategically adopting the first-person plural to address her fellow Australian readers, Veronica argues that

> the Mabo decision blurs the distinctions we had drawn between ourselves and the aborigines, writing them back into a history from which we had written them out, and suggesting that our unity may not be as monolithic as we think.[25]

Chief among those distinctions is the binary opposition between primitive and civilised society, with its normative corollaries of wildness and law, evil and good. She argues that these assumptions and beliefs are derived from myths and symbols inherited from pre-modern or early modern Europe and have shaped the pre-understandings of white Australians. As a consequence, the *Mabo* decision 'strikes at the root of our self-definition as a people'.[26]

Except in the case of Antarctica, the phrase *terra nullius* is a figure of legal speech that has shaped Australian settler understandings of space not only at the political, but also at the personal, level. What Behrendt calls a 'psychological *terra nullius*' amounts to an embodied ideology or shared 'structure of feeling' in Raymond Williams's terminology.[27] It is a theory of Australian space, and this becomes the focus of Veronica's analysis. For her own theorised account, Veronica draws on a the comparative religionists Raimundo Panikkar and Mircea Eliade, who argued that 'there is no outer without inner space, without some transformation of physical fact into psychic reality'.[28]

---

24. Mark Davis, *The Land of Plenty: Australia in the 2000s* (Melbourne: Melbourne University Press, 2008), 62.
25. Brady, 'Mabo', 14. In the article the name of the case is not italicised.
26. Brady, 'Mabo', 13.
27. Raymond Williams, *Marxism and Literature* (London: Chatto and Windus, 1977), 129.
28. Brady, 'Mabo', 13, quoting Panikkar, 'There Is No Outer without Inner Space', in *Cross-Currents*, 43/1 (1993): 60–81.

This cross-cultural perspective decentres European assumptions by creating a framework that is inclusive of Aboriginal understandings of space. The 'psychic reality' or perceptual framework underlying *terra nullius* was a reductive, geometric idea that space, especially in the non-European parts of the world, was 'an emptiness waiting to be filled'.[29] White Australians, as the heirs of colonisation, have also inherited this scientific rationalist view of space as 'physical fact', and have consequently 'tended to live only in physical space, for economic purposes'. By contrast, Aboriginal culture sees the land in terms of a cosmos in which spiritual and physical dimensions are integrated, and in which every place is associated with story and law. As a result, 'people and land lived in a symbiotic and mutually supportive relationship'.

It is interesting that in developing this argument Veronica does not invoke the common theoretical distinction between space and place, presumably because it would have muddied the conceptual distinction she wished to make between a secular and instrumentalist understanding of land as resource and an Indigenous understanding of land as sacred.[30] Veronica derives her account of the experiential dimension of the colonisers' understanding from literature, particularly from Marcus Clarke's account of the 'weird melancholy' of the Australian bush:

> All that the newcomers saw were the 'strange scribblings of nature learning how to write' . . . But the Aborigines belonged there, and could read the Book of Nature closed to the settlers. So, imaginatively, they were subsumed into this vacancy and into the dread it provoked.[31]

Discerning an essential continuity between the construction of the Aboriginal in colonial writing and the arguments of opponents of *Mabo*, Veronica unites an understanding of colonialism as an ongoing structure of territorial acquisition and a psychoanalytic reading

---

29. Brady, 'Mabo', 14.
30. She does use this distinction in later articles, such as 'Aboriginal Spirituality', in *Literature and Theology*, 10/3 (1996): 242–51, and 'Journey into the Land', in *Changing Places: Re-Imagining Australia*, edited by John Cameron (Double Bay: Longueville Books, 2003), 264–71.
31. Brady, 'Mabo', 16, quoting Marcus Clarke, 'Preface to the Poems of Adam Lindsay Gordon.'

of the Indigene as abjected other, the Wild Man of the European imaginary.[32] While this argument occludes variable relations to place among European Australians in order to expound the deep cultural and psychic roots of this Manichean Allegory, Veronica does explicitly recognise the possibility of change, of reconciliation between these opposites.

While such hope is undoubtedly a part of her theology, it also emerges from her understanding of the way symbols work: 'To the extent that [ideology] relies on symbols which govern the process of imagining ourselves and our world, symbols may hold the key to change.'[33] Here the role of the literary imagination is vital: just as literary texts have articulated the dominant symbols of colonialism, so they may 'renew the symbols by which we live'. In the final section of her paper, Veronica demonstrates this self-reflexive and creative work on inherited symbols in fictional narrative through a reading of David Malouf's *Remembering Babylon*.

Published in 1993, *Remembering Babylon* is set in the early decades of the colony of Queensland, and centres on a frontier community's treatment of Gemmy Fairley, a white man who has been living for sixteen years with an Aboriginal group, and who suddenly appears atop the fence that divides the cleared lands from the wilderness. Gemmy, that is to say, is a liminal figure, whose identity challenges the binary of self and other on which colonial ideology rested. Initially offered hospitality as a rescued white man, he soon provokes unease and suspicion as an ally or agent of the blacks. For Veronica, Malouf's representation of the terror that Gemmy arouses by crossing the line the settlers have drawn between 'civilisation' and 'wilderness' has 'a contemporary parallel in the panic Mabo has occasioned'.[34] More than this, the novel traces through later experiences of the children who first met Gemmy at the boundary fence some of the after-effects of that encounter: in Janet it is an openness to the sacred, to 'a more polyphonic sense of self and world,' while in Lachlan it is an occasion of sorrow, an intuition of lost opportunity, which Veronica reads as a form of guilt in the sense defined

---

32. I draw here on the work of Patrick Wolfe, 'Nation and MiscegeNation: Discursive Continuity in the Post-Mabo Era', in *Social Analysis*, 36 (October 1994): 93–152.
33. Brady, 'Mabo', 22.
34. Brady, 'Mabo', 23.

by Ricoeur, of 'feeling responsible for not being responsible'.[35] As a result, these characters move mentally beyond the 'fearful enclosure of colonial society' to recognise the humanity of the other and their claims to justice. For Veronica, this realisation parallels the contemporaneous recognition of the Aboriginal relationship to land in the legal sphere:

> The Mabo decision points to one way of beginning to right these historic wrongs, a way to begin to move . . . into the rich, more polyphonic sense of reality characteristic of Aboriginal culture.

In *Can These Bones Live?* Veronica had drawn on Clifford Geertz's symbolic anthropology to argue that 'history is largely "traffic in significant symbols".'[36] Her reading of the fence symbol in *Remembering Babylon* as a border was an astute and courageous intervention in the context of the *Mabo* backlash. Fences constitute a virtual declaration of private property in Western society, and their potent symbolism had been deployed by the mining industry in an infamous poster showing Aboriginal people building a wall across the state of Western Australia.[37] By representing the fence in conjunction with a liminal figure, Malouf critically examines its psychosocial functions and the ethics of the ideology of property. The character of Gemmy is itself a trope that draws on historical figures such as William Buckley, James Murrell, known as Jemmy, Eliza Fraser and Barbara Thompson, runaway convicts or shipwrecked castaways who lived with Aboriginal people for years before returning to white society, and who have entered Australian folklore. Malouf's construction of Gemmy was critiqued as a signifier of proxy Aboriginality by Germaine Greer, an interpretation more rigorously pursued by Suvendrini Perera, who argued that the novel presents 'a discourse of happy hybridisation'.[38] Offering a materialist postcolonial reading

---

35. Brady, 'Mabo', 27.
36. Brady, *Can These Bones Live?*, 7, quoting Geertz, *The Interpretation of Cultures* (New York: Basic Books, 1973), 45.
37. Reference to be supplied—if I can find one.
38. Suvendrini Perera, 'Unspeakable Bodies: Representing the Aboriginal in Australian Critical Discourse', in *Meridian* 13 (1994): 17.

of the imagery of hybridity associated with Janet and Gemmy, Perera concluded that the novel provides an 'easy answer to troubled questions of identity posed by settler societies' and 'erases the complexities of the process for its indigenous subjects'.[39] While this is a cogent reading that critically questions the innovativeness of Malouf's symbolism, it is also worth noting that *Remembering Babylon* has continued to attract new analyses of the settler community's response to Gemmy.[40] This focus leads me to reflect on how the space between the two cultures materialises through the arrival of Gemmy, creating opportunities for exchange as well as suspicion and domination. In this respect, Veronica correctly discerned the parallels between *Remembering Babylon* and *Mabo*. In 1997 the Aboriginal lawyer Noel Pearson argued that native title was a 'recognition concept', that is, one that was not a common law title or an Aboriginal law title, but rather one belonging 'to the space between the two systems of law', and affording the recognition of Aboriginal property rights by Anglo-Australian law 'in particular circumstances'.[41] Gemmy also functions as a figure for this 'in-between' space, or what anthropologists Benjamin R Smith and Frances Morphy in a commentary on Pearson's concept call 'the overlap between distinct fields'.[42] As such, Gemmy signals the possibility of mediation, but ultimately becomes a scapegoat. Pearson's rider about the availability of native title being limited to 'particular circumstances' has been confirmed as subsequent court cases have shown the limits of this 'recognition'. All of this suggests that there is an idealistic element to the construction of Gemmy, but as Paul Ricoeur noted, utopian imaginings represent

39. Perera, 'Unspeakable Bodies', 19.
40. See in particular Victoria Burrows, 'The Ghostly haunting of White Shame in David Malouf's *Remembering Babylon*', in *Westerly*, 51 (2006): 124–35. See also Nicolette Bragg, 'Between Dwelling and Belonging: The Hospitality of David Malouf's *Remembering Babylon*', in *Cultural Studies Review*, 21 (2015): 2055–22.
41. Noel Pearson, 'The Concept of Native Title at Common Law', *Australian Humanities Review* 5 (1997). http://www.australianhumanitiesreview.org/archive/Issue-March-1997/pearson.html
42. Benjamin R Smith and Frances Morphy, 'The Social Effects of Native Title', in *The Social Effects of Native Title: Recognition, Translation, Coexistence*, edited by Benjamin Smith and Frances Morphy (Canberra: ANU E-Press, 2007), 5.

'a symbolic opening towards the future.'[43] The literary is a space for imagining justice beyond that achievable in law.

Veronica continued to work to bring about the 'symbolic opening' she had discerned in *Mabo*, through her writings and other aspects of her life, in particular devoting herself to the study of Aboriginal literature and theology.[44] A key feature of her method, as prominent in 'Mabo: A Question of Space' as elsewhere, is her eclectic approach to symbolic interpretation. She juxtaposes references to Ricoeur and Lacan, Eliade and Said, Arendt and Hayden White. This interdisciplinary breadth was a crucial element in her success as a lecturer and as a public intellectual, as it showed humanities research being put to work in the clarification of social realities. It allowed her to see beneath the surface to deeper connections and meanings. At times the juxtapositions surprise, such as when she cites the Jungian Mircea Eliade on the 'ceremonial taking possession of new territory' in the course of a critique of colonial authority that draws on Homi Bhabha.[45] There is no postcolonial consciousness in the original source, and although Veronica is appropriating it for those ends, the colonial-legal origins of the metaphor of possession stand out in the context of *Mabo* and native title.[46] Such a 'heterogeneous repertoire' of critical tools gives to the form of Veronica's writing a sense of *bricolage*, in that they are applied in relation to a variety of cultural contexts and critical projects. It is tempting to suggest a fundamental affinity between this style and the mythic and theological nature of her world-view. Lévi-Strauss noted in *The Savage Mind* that 'Mythical thought is . . . a kind of intellectual *bricolage*', relating it to the motivated sign systems that tended to characterise such societies in contrast to the more arbitrary sign systems that characterise mod-

---

43. Paul Ricoeur, 'The Creativity of Language', in *A Ricoeur Reader: Reflection and Imagination*, edited Mario J Valdès (Toronto: University of Toronto Press, 1991), 475.
44. See especially 'Thinking about Feeling: Bill Neidjie's *Story About Feeling*', in *Caught in the Draught*, 38–49, and 'Aboriginal Spirituality', in *Literature and Theology*, 10/3 (1996): 242–51.
45. See Brady, 'Mabo', 25.
46. Mircea Eliade, *The Myth of the Eternal Return*, translated by Willard R Trask (New York: Pantheon books, 1954), 10.

ern societies.[47] Yet, as her recommendation to me of John Caputo's *Prayers and Tears of Jacques Derrida* shows, Veronica was as much committed to the traditions of *logos* as to those of *mythos*. Derrida himself, in his response to Lévi-Strauss, suggested that 'every discourse is *bricoleur*,' and perhaps this is especially true of the interdisciplinary and intercultural studies that Veronica modelled, in which 'theology involves a social critique,' and literary symbols express a 'longing for justice.[48]

---

47. Claude Lévi-Strauss, *The Savage Mind* (1962; Chicago: University of Chicago Press, 1966), 19.
48. Jacques Derrida, *Writing and Difference*, translated by Alan Bass (London: Routledge, 1978), 285, qtd Jeremy Hawthorn, *A Concise Glossary of Contemporary Literary Theory* (London: Edward Arnold, 1992), 14.

The Future of the University and the Politics of Conviction

Leigh Dale

Inspired by the teaching and research of Veronica Brady, my aim is to consider the culture of humanities teaching in Australian universities, to talk about how we read stories and how reading can make a difference. These are things Veronica was concerned with, and her views are encapsulated in an essay drawn to my attention by Susan Sheridan, a fellow scholar of Australian literature:

> The pattern of meanings in our culture, however, being determinedly secular, has tended to turn its symbols into signs, limiting their implications to those dictated by journalists, politicians and economists. Thinking beyond these economic and pragmatic premises is thus regarded with suspicion, as somehow non-intellectual, certainly not hard-headed.[1]

'Intellectual Belief and Freedom' was published in the Melbourne journal *Meanjin* in 1991. Veronica's argument, that intellectuals need to think beyond the literal, the instrumental and the simplistic, is inspiring, but prompts the question, *how* might we do this? How to move from sign to symbol, as Veronica urges us to do, or more simply, from considering or relying on literal meanings, to opening up to poetic ones, to complicate rather than to resort to slogans? My main focus today is universities and their narrative patterns, but I'll begin and end by referring to a novel, Timothy Findley's *Not Wanted on the Voyage* (1984).

Not Wanted on the Voyage takes up the story of Noah and the ark told in some early chapters of the book of Genesis. In Findley's wildly

---

1. Veronica Brady, 'Intellectual Belief and Freedom', in *Meanjin,* 50 (1991): 535.

re-imagined account Noah becomes 'Dr Noah Noyes', a man more inclined to say 'no' than 'yes', unlike his wife who is given to spontaneous and sometimes dangerous acts of compassion. The novel endorses Mrs Noyes' perspective, and it begins like this:

> Everyone knows it wasn't like that.

> To begin with, they make it sound as if there wasn't any argument; as if there wasn't any panic—no one being pushed aside—no one being trampled—none of the animals howling—none of the people screaming blue murder. They make it sound as if the only people who wanted to get on board were Doctor Noyes and his family. Presumably, everyone else (the rest of the human race, so to speak) stood off waving gaily, behind a distant barricade: SPECTATORS WILL NOT CROSS THE YELLOW LINE and: THANK YOU FOR YOUR COOPERATION. With all the baggage neatly labelled: WANTED or NOT WANTED ON THE VOYAGE.[2]

Findley's novel is usually read as a fable about the politics of inclusiveness—who is, and who is not, allowed 'on board'. Outside of fiction, the brutal tragedy of exclusion is being played out across the planet, and the situation is overwhelming: the United Nations at the end of 2014 estimated there were nearly sixty million people who were either refugees or internally displaced.[3] Amidst this chaos, and the violence that underpins it, the mere existence of a school or a university is a triumph. Former ABC radio announcer Emma Ayres, now teaching music in Afghanistan's capital city Kabul, was asked in an interview last year 'how much . . . anxiety do you carry day-to-day?' She said that though she tries to be 'sensible' and 'aware', it was not really feasible constantly to be anxious, given her decision to live in Afghanistan; the alternative was to be a 'nervous wreck'.[4] The ques-

---

2. Timothy Findley, *Not Wanted on the Voyage* (Toronto: Viking, 1984; reprinted Penguin, 1985), 1.

3. The UNHCR estimates around 1/3 of these people are displaced beyond national borders, with nearly 40 million displaced within their own country. See: <www.unhcr.org.uk/about-us/key-facts-and-figures.html>.

4. Emma Ayres, 'Making Music in Kabul', ABC *Sunday Extra* at <www.abc.net.au/radionational/programs/sundayextra/sunday-extra-02.07.2015/6640228#>. Accessed 1 February 2016.

tion of how to live with the constant threat of military level violence was also raised in an ABC story on the attack on Bacha Khan University in Pakistan in January 2016. Retired army officer Brigadier Said Nazir, interviewed by Ashraf Ali, remarked that 'the offensive capability of the attackers always frustrates the defensive mechanism of the state . . . *because the threat can never be accurately measured*' (emphasis added).[5] In the case of Bacha Khan University, named after a pacifist hero of Pakistan, the main entrance to the university was heavily fortified but, under the cover of fog, the gunmen entered by the unguarded rear gate.

I have two reasons for mentioning the global context. The first is to acknowledge that for people like Emma Ayres or the students of Bacha Khan University, trying to think about policy problems in higher education or literary criticism might seem solipsistic, even callous. Our difficulty is to keep different kinds of scale in view, taking responsibility for the local whilst maintaining the sense of proportion that acknowledges global contexts and radical inequalities. And referring to the violence of war and terrorism is also a way of giving some perspective to what I perceive as the disproportionate level of fear and anxiety in Australian life, particularly in and around the workplace. My data or proof of this is a bit patchy: Christos Tsiolkas's novel *The Slap*, in which character after character erupts in anger over trivial matters, and the popularity of the television series which took up this story; the conversations I hear while students are waiting for class, in which stress is a constant theme; and what I read and see and hear in workplaces, of those frustrated, debilitated and demeaned by the pressure not to deliver services (treat others well) but to tick boxes and eliminate (often wildly unrealistic or exaggerated) threats of litigation. The main fear seems to be of losing one's job, while jobs are constantly being made harder to do as fear begets a desire for an irrational level of control. I read Australia's abhorrent (and ineffective) response to those seeking asylum as an *extension* of this underlying cycle. Put simply, not only is the hyperinflation of panic proportionate or effective in meeting the challenges we face,

---

5. Ashraf Ali, 'Bacha Khan University: Schools under attack as Taliban vows to kill Pakistan's future leaders "in their nurseries"' at <www.abc.net.au/news/2016-01-28/talibans-war-on-education-as-hundreds-of-schools-blown-up/7119008>. Accessed 1 February 2016.

the discordant and disproportionate focus on being seen to play by the rules is actively damaging and distorting the provision of services.

This cycle of fear, regulation and control seems more evident in the public sector than in the private, with idiotic levels of over-regulation and panic-stricken changes of policy seemingly driven by an irrational belief that well-run institutions can prepare for every contingency. The current popularity of the phrase 'future-proofing' for example shows the seductive power of metaphor, that entire institutions led by intelligent people are able persuade themselves they can predict and respond adequately to, say, climate change or political turmoil; linked is the equally seductive fiction that by establishing micro-level mechanisms of regulation and surveillance, such institutions can maintain legitimacy and thus justify public funding. But Anne-Marie Cummins asserts that 'the desire to know' enacted in quality assurance masks a deeper desire *not* to know things which are uncomfortable, unsettling and most definitely not reassuring' (emphasis added).[6] Cummins, a social psychologist, believes that universities in the United Kingdom have been, and I quote, 'internally colonised by quality assurance regimes': taken over by endless checking that everything is alright, such that the actual core functions of teaching and research are no longer conducted in ways that respond either to student need or norms established by the relevant discipline. Such control and monitoring function to reassure the public there is no problem. They are designed to take little account of evidence to the contrary—indeed, at times it seems that they take little account of evidence at all. It is very useful to remember this desire *not* to know when trying to interpret the behaviour, words, and guiding documents of federal and institutional policy-makers: the desire to hear only the voice that cries 'all's well'. Done well, planning, oversight and review are useful processes. But pushed into absurd detail, preparation for unlikely worst-case scenarios can risk infantilising all who participate in the workplace, whether as managers, workers or those receiving services. Perhaps the most debilitating element of this cultural shift of the last twenty years is that it prefabricates bad faith: in endlessly designing policies and procedures which presume

---

6. Anne-Marie, Cummins, '"The road to hell is paved with good intentions": Quality Assurance as Social Defence against Anxiety', in *Organizational and Social Dynamics,* 2/1 (2002): 100.

incompetence and litigiousness, we are distorting service delivery and institutional function. Just as insidiously, failure of policy design and high-level decision-making is devolved onto individuals charged with frontline service delivery. The intensity and punitive potential of scrutiny (culminating in dismissal) always seems function in inverse proportion to actual decision-making power.

What Cummins identities as a fire blanket designed to perpetu-ate the falsehood that institutions are functioning to a high level is a far cry from the culture of interrogation which prevailed at the University of Queensland in May 1981. Students ridiculed attempts by academics to gain control of the English Department committee, which had a student majority. This committee had oversight of teach-ing; frustrated by student dominance of that committee, academics called a meeting which excluded them, prompting the circulation of this poster:

As a legacy of this culture, when I started teaching at the University of Queensland in 1996 we were not allowed to put assessment infor-mation into our subject outlines, because the form and weighting of assessment had to be discussed with students. Twenty years later, the subject outline is everywhere regarded as a contract between insti-tution and student which cannot be changed regardless of circum-stances (for example non-arrival of textbooks from the publisher). At one level this is frustrating—if a class is struggling, academics find it difficult to slow down; if it needs to be challenged more, academics are limited in what they can add. One frustrated head of school mentioned in despair that a subject outline he was reading had ballooned to more than fifty pages, so thorough were its warnings about what might go wrong and how to cope if it did. The main problem raised by the obsession with 'risk management' and its manifestation in the frameworks of teaching and learning, particularly as it relates to the functioning of subjects, is the gap between the predictability of form, and the volatility and challenge of the world students are said to walk into on graduation, but which, of course, *they already inhabit*. The question arises: are all these mechanisms designed to ensure quality of teaching working, or is their function to reassure us that it *is* working when it might not be? This is what Cummins would argue, and there are other grounds to suggest that indeed, all is not well in universities.

As is generally well known, successive and serious reductions of funding to Australian universities took place first in the late 1980s under higher education minister John Dawkins. Dawkins vowed to create a 'Unified National System', which would do away with distinctions between colleges, institutes of technology, and universities. Per capita funding for tertiary institutions was set halfway between the level enjoyed by colleges and universities, leading to an effective ten percent cut for universities, who had been charged with conducting research implicitly of a more theoretical and general nature than that undertaken by institutes of technology. The savings were transferred to newly named universities; in the institution in which I was working at the time, many staff, never tasked with research and unqualified to perform it, either embarked on the intimidating project of attempting to gain a PhD whilst holding down a full time job (often late in their career), or took a redundancy package. On very my first day on that job, there was a notice in my pigeonhole—a slip of paper courteously distributed to everyone in the faculty—offering me a redundancy. It was a sobering start to an academic career. In 1996, on the election of the Liberal-National Party coalition, John Howard's 'razor gang' carved another thick slice from university budgets; a more recent attack by Labor, euphemised as an 'efficiency dividend' of 3.5% (a figure made larger by general increases in salaries and other costs), has also taken a heavy toll. Some sense of the state and scale of the problem can be gained by comparing current funding with that achieved under Menzies.

Funding of Australian Higher Education[7]

	1957	2014–16
Proportion of federal budget to universities	2.7%	2.1%
Federal government spending as a proportion of university budgets	31.3% + 39.8%[8]	c 40%
Student numbers	30 000	1 000 000
Student fees as a proportion of university budgets	13%	19% (+ 17% overseas students)

I have used the 1950s as a benchmark because the Murray committee inquiry (1957) found Australian universities 'overcrowded, short staffed, poorly housed and under equipped'.[9] (Most writers benchmark against the 1970s, the high watermark of federal funding, reached under Gough Whitlam's Labor government.) As another measure of decline, Abbott and Doucouliagos suggest that per capita student funding more than halved between 1977 and 2001.[10] And it is worth noting the difference of sentiment under Menzies, compared to the present day: in the 1950s, Colombo plan scholarships brought thousands of overseas students to Australian universities[11];

---

7. Budget Projection 2015–16 from <http://budget.gov.au/2014–15/content/bp1/html/bp1_bst6-01.htm>. Accessed 2 February 2016. Proportion of domestic student fees calculated from 'Finance 2014: Financial Reports of Higher Education Providers' at <https://docs.education.gov.au/node/38416>. Accessed 2 February 2016. Student numbers for 2015 from Universities Australia, 'Key Facts and Data' at <www.universitiesaustralia.edu.au/australias-universities/key-facts-and-data#.VqwnE6O4bX4>. Accessed 2 February 2016. Figures for 1950 spending from Malcolm Abbott and Chris Doucouliagos, 'The Changing Structure of Higher Education in Australia 1949–2003' at <www.deakin.edu.au/__data/assets/pdf_file/0006/402594/swp2003_07.pdf>. Accessed 2 February 2016.
8. States supplied nearly 40% of funding, as universities had been established by acts of colonial, thence state, parliaments.
9. Abbott and Doucouliagos, 'The Changing Structure of Higher Education in Australia 1949–2003', 5.
10. Abbott and Doucouliagos, 'The Changing Structure of Higher Education in Australia 1949–2003', 25.
11. Abbott and Doucouliagos, 'The Changing Structure of Higher Education in Australia 1949–2003', 5.

these days, most overseas students pay significant fees, money that is crucial to the operation of the Australian system given the costs of teaching and research.

One element of this increase is the seven billion dollars now spent annually on non-academic staff. The tragedy for this group, often over-worked, *is* that they are overworked, often on the development, promotion and policing of those systems of regulation noted above. The other big systemic change observable from this table is of scale: universities in Australia now teach more than one million students. Whilst on the one hand this might be taken as an economic neces-sity—those who are students are not looking for work, something very handy for governments—my suspicion is that so many tertiary students work such long hours that a diminution in the number of tertiary places might cause less of a spike in unemployment than might be thought. One might *also* assume that because we have more universities and many more students in them, that there would be more diversity in subjects and approaches. This is not the case in Aus-tralia in relation to the study of literature. Doing a survey of English programs a couple of years ago, I was surprised by the uniformity in structure—we look more like the 1950s, when universities were virtually uniform, than the 1970s when the diversification of curricu-lum and the establishment of distinctive institutional identities was dramatically accelerated.[12] We have in English a 'standard' first-year package, something that also exists across almost all humanities dis-ciplines. This reflects the orthodoxy that there should be scaffolding of subjects based on hierarchies of knowledge. This is not necessarily a bad idea . . . unless we are speaking of an area like English, where the very idea of hierarchy has been under challenge for the last half cen-tury, and where debate about significance *constitutes* the discipline.

I should not have been surprised by seeing such a peculiarly timid and 'generic' version of the discipline, for the institutional shape of most (perhaps all) humanities disciplines has been pared and pruned in accordance with orthodoxies about the optimal size of what are now called 'programs' (rather than disciplines): one or two full-time academics delivering lectures and convening subjects, with tutorial groups taken by casual staff. As Gaye Tuchman has pointed out in her

---

12. Leigh Dale, 'Reading English?', in *Australian Literary Studies* 28/1–2 (2013): 1–14.

book *Wannabe U*, as higher education has transformed from service to industry, universities are inclined to 'innovate' in unison, not least because senior managers who have implemented change (or are able to claim to have done so) are recruited by rivals to make the same changes, reflecting the shared belief of senior managers that 'their own activities define the essence of the university'.[13] These institutional identities are sketched by administrators, confected by marketers, then expressed through 'branding', rather than being built from the ground up on the basis of actual achievements in research and/ or teaching.

One response to this diminution of funding, acute since Dawkins, and the shift towards management control over disciplinary configuration, has been a high rate of *structural* change as disciplines (or 'programs') are merged, re-located and renamed. Often promoted as flexibility or responsiveness to demand, the constant flux in institutional mission at the level of undergraduate teaching, badged as 'renewal', almost always turns out to be job cuts. The instability and the lack of substance underpinning the creation and promotion of institutional identities has become a serious cultural issue: the high level thinking that underlies the best teaching and research, like high performance in sport, demands equanimity and confidence, as it also demands (in the simplest sense) long lead times. It is not clear why we should expect survivors of endless restructures, rebrandings, mergers and relocations, not to mention forced redundancies, to believe they are working in harmony with their institution's goals, or that they should spend serious time developing advanced level subjects which might never taught because students who begin with a specific set of rules are unlikely to graduate under the same conditions. Not surprisingly, changes are often resisted on the basis of loyalty to disciplinary paradigms; this resistance if usually reconfigured as inflexibility, ignorance, or old age, when in fact it is underpinned by a demand for exactly that 'rational' thinking said to underpin the need to change.

In a wonderful 'Dilbert' cartoon, Scott Adams writes of a workplace announcement that 'we're hiring a Director of Change Management to help employees embrace strategic changes', to which Dilbert responds, 'or we could come up with strategies that make sense, then

---

13. Gaye Tuchman, *Wannabe U: Inside the Corporate University* (Chicago: The University of Chicago Press, 2009), 6.

employees would embrace change'.[14] But my favourite fictional execu-
tive position is from the BBC television series *W1A*, a program about
the BBC which features (fanfare) a Director of Better. More seriously,
I note that the University of Western Australia's 'change management' documents seek to represent resistance as a kind of emotional
dysfunction, whilst themselves being somewhat contradictory. The
foreword to the overview document, 'A Guide for Leaders and Management' says this: 'The root of most resistance is emotional, therefore the solution must address these emotions through empathy,
information and engagement.' In a section titled 'Understanding the
difference between change and transition'—a difference too subtle for
this literary critic to understand—we read:

> No matter how beneficial the change might be, or how clearly
> it is communicated, employee resistance to change can occur.
> You will inevitably encounter some degree of resistance from
> someone on your team, whether or not they vocalise their
> objections. Resistance can be particularly damaging because
> it can decrease productivity and can also increase turnover.
> While it is difficult to prevent resistance altogether, there
> are some strategies you can utilise to help get your team on
> board.
>
> Most changes fail. In a Harvard Business Review study, 66%
> of change initiatives failed to achieve their desired business
> outcomes (Harvard Business Review, 2009). Change can
> be unsettling, even good change. Employees are constantly
> experiencing changes in their careers, and these impact on
> employee productivity and retention.

If 'most changes fail' and 'change builds resilience', then it is not clear
why 'change'—the university's preferred term for the loss of 300 jobs
and the appointment of fifty new academic staff, preceded as it was
by a round of voluntary redundancies, should be expected to have the
claimed outcomes, nor indeed why the logic of resistance should be
reframed as 'emotional'. The glorious part of this document is its last
line, part of a self-checking process that managers can use to monitor
whether they are leading change well. They are asked to tick a box,
'Yes' or 'No', to the question 'Am I telling the truth?' The first ques-

---

14. <www.pinterest.com/pin/517421444658036278/>. Accessed 1 February 2016.

tion is 'Have I accepted the fact that non-stop change is the unavoidable reality today, or am I still fighting it?' One wonders what kind of knowledge underpins such a claim, or whether the volatile and ineffective 'change' is garnering attention in order to avoid a systematic consideration of how to combat chronic underfunding.

At this point, I want to turn back to literature, and to literary studies, to consider the question of how the high-level reading taught and demonstrated by Veronica Brady might be part of our critique of this thinking. To do this, the first step is to move past the irritation we might feel at documents (or their authors) who reframe critique itself—*intrinsic to the functioning of a university*—as dysfunction. How can disciplinary practices in literary studies be part of the response to challenge and replace such thinking with more effective ways to approach diminished funding?[15] And what are those 'disciplinary practices'—what do scholars of literature actually do?

Whilst I have been studying literature for thirty-five years, I still find it difficult to answer this last question clearly, so I want to use an analogy with music, which begins by explaining what I cannot do when I listen to music. Because I have the capacity to hear, I can listen to any form of music, and I can have a response—sing along, offer criticisms, be moved, turn the radio off because I don't like the song or symphony. I can do these things without having even a basic understanding of the formal elements that underpin composition or performance or musical genres. Sharps and flats, E and C, let alone the rules that govern their selection, are all a mystery to me and yes I *should* have paid attention to Miss Draper in Year Eight when she tried to explain these things but I didn't, or perhaps I just couldn't understand. Contrast my incapacity to *hear* (as opposed to listen) with that of a player in one of Australia's leading orchestras. She made a remark about performance that prompted me to ask whether she could hear every instrument when the orchestra was playing. Glancing down modestly, she said, 'Yeah. Yeah, I can'. I cannot imagine being able to hear every note made by every instrument at all times, and I certainly do not pretend to discern every element of a written

---

15. Some outstanding examples are Christopher Newfield's *Ivy and Industry: Business and the Making of the American University* (Durham and London: Duke University Press, 2003) and *Unmaking the Public University: The Forty-year Assault on the Middle Class* (Boston: Harvard University Press, 2008), along with Frank Donoghue's *The Last Professors*.

text. But I can understand something of the form of literary works, *how* books 'make their sounds', how these sounds—words, narrative patterns, structures of stories—connect to cultural patterns, or seek to break with them. Anyone who is able to read can read a book; trained readers, *and* writers, notice elements of form, *how* a text speaks or works, that others might not.

Good readers can understand the cruelty and cunning of metaphor, as well as its beauty and novelty; understand the cultural significance of specific words, like 'colonisation' or 'invasion'; understand the need to use words correctly; and draw attention to the challenges laid down by literary works, whether Judith Wright's *Generations of Men* or Gail Jones' *Sorry*, both written not 'ahead of time', but *against* the times as challenges to the culture of colonial supremacy. Such literary works aim to forge new pathways of story, and this forging is often painful for writer and reader. It is often met with strong resistance. Such books bring us to new ways of thinking, not least by showing the moral inadequacy of some ways of speaking and forging the pathways of new stories. And reading such works changes people, because they think differently about past, present, and future. Reading of such works, whether it is done in a classroom or by those who have been in classrooms, helps to mediate and promote deepened understanding of books like those by Jones and Wright; it is a public good. The scholarly teaching of the reading of literature is part of the push for complexity, nuance, and depth of knowledge, against glibness, falsity and bad faith.

The notion of the public good was under threat when Veronica published her *Meanjin* essay in 1991. Under then minister of higher education John Dawkins, also a UWA graduate I'm sorry to say, the view became fashionable that a university education was a *private* good, not a public one. Seen this way—as a benefit to the individual—a university degree again became something for which the individual should pay, as it was in the early part of the twentieth century. Such a change is never just financial, it is also, always, cultural; it positions 'higher learning' as a commodity, something to *buy*, rather than 'the student experience' as something to *be*. Such instrumentalist and individualist views constantly challenge the German notion of *Bildung*, the formation of the self that is the theme of the *Bildungsroman*, the novel of education, which *also* has been part of the formation and function of the modern university since the early nineteenth century, particularly in Arts faculties. But as Christopher Newfield shows, such beliefs have *always* been challenged, by those who believe that universities should only teach 'useful' subjects because they accept public funding (Newfield, *Unmaking* and *Ivy and Industry*; Dale, *Enchantment*).[16] Since Dawkins, the instrumentalists have been on top.

One of the things Veronica insisted on with reading was that we should move from part to whole—from context, understood in its broadest sense, to the detail of word and sentence. Whilst this kind of reading is sometimes called 'historicist', by which is meant understanding literary texts in terms of a specific moment in time, Veronica's term was 'hermeneutics'. This word evokes a rich tradition of religious scholarship, but I think now it was also in some sense idealist, in the specific sense that Veronica always insisted (when teaching) that as readers we should not just think about what *is*, but reflect on what might be. Of course her term also took for granted a constructivist view, the notion that that culture—hence meaning and value—are not intrinsic to cultural forms but are *made*, not least through debate in university classrooms but perhaps most importantly by great works of literature. Her passionately materialist views about the economic bases of society were brought into conjunction with a more subtle but perhaps ultimately more powerfully held belief in the importance of the non-material to our intellectual and emotional being. Veronica's attention to material context and symbolic meaning helped to counter the fact that the centre of gravity of most stories is an individual, inviting readings which operate at that scale: do I like this character, do I not. Is what this book says about this person true of me and people I know? The habit of reading for the individual is very ingrained, and the focus on the individual is often, implicitly, an invitation to celebrate the *agency* of the individual, exemplified in the Nike slogan 'just do it' and which we see here in the photograph of Oscar Pistorius which configures this agency as masculine and militaristic:

---

16. Newfield, *Ivy and Industry: Business and the Making of the American University*; Newfield, *Unmaking the Public University: The Forty-year Assault on the Middle Class*; Leigh Dale, *The Enchantment of English: Professing Literature in Australian Universities* (Sydney: Sydney University Press, 2012).

(Hayward)[17]

What Karl Marx calls 'the sheet lightning of the daily press,'[18] to which we can add television and the internet, spotlights the individual, uses the individual as the centrepiece of stories. Noticing the rhetorical use of the individual is a useful first step in thinking about why there is resistance to thinking about complex issues: the collective good, forces larger than the individual, forces we cannot control. I take this point from Joan Didion, who suggests that the media is obsessed with individuals, as long as they were nice folk or, if not, easily slotted into categories for not nice.[19] Didion argues that this happens because stories about individuals not only reinforce the belief in singularity and power—particularly white male power—that we see in the Nike advertisment, but because using a smaller scale allows writers and readers to *avoid* the challenge of thinking about social structures.[20] In her evocative words, rather than thinking about politics or economics or social forces, it is more seductive to frame social issues in terms of the experiences of a peculiarly homogenised individual:

17. Paul Hayward, 'Man, not superman: an idol falls', in *Sydney Morning Herald* 16 Feb. 2013: <www.smh.com.au/world/man-not-superman-an-idol-falls-20130215-2eign.htm>, l. Accessed 1 February 2016.

18. Karl Marx, 'The Eighteenth Brumaire of Louis Bonaparte', 1852 at: <www.marxists.org/archive/marx/works/1852/18th-brumaire/ch01.htm>. Accessed 2 February 2016.

19. Joan Didion, 'Sentimental Journeys', in *New York Review of Books,* 28 (1991).

20. Louis Menand, 'Out of Bethlehem: The Radicalization of Joan Didion', in *New Yorker* 24 August 2015: <www.nybooks.com.ezproxy.uow.edu.au/issues/>. Accessed 29 January 2016.

> Lady Liberty, huddled masses, ticker-tape parades, heroes,
> gutters, bright lights, broken hearts, eight million stories in
> the naked city; eight million stories and all the same story,
> each devised to obscure not only the city's actual tensions
> of race and class but also, more significantly, the civic and
> commercial arrangements that rendered those tensions
> irreconcilable.

In this quote from her essay 'Sentimental Journeys', you can see that Joan Didion and Anne-Marie Cummins, the psychologist mentioned earlier, work from similar premises: that focusing on the literal meaning can disguise the symbolic and psychological significance of how stories are told and what they obscure. Let me suggest that another function of constantly stressing individual agency, whether in relation to power or pathology, whether in discussing universities and their benefits or in popular culture, is to disguise the fact individuals have so *little* power. Imagine, at this very moment, forty Australian university marketing departments all intent on assuring one million students that each is valued as an individual.

Brigadier Nazir spoke of the difficulty of measuring risk: how to measure and prepare for the likelihood of being shot when lecturing in Chemistry at Bacha Khan University, as Syed Hamid Hussain was, or being shot when about to take an English exam, as Haider Ali was. The main risk to higher education in Australia is probably not violence, nor even being sued for failing to instil the graduate attribute or learning outcome mandated by a subject outline. The greatest risk academics and students face is from forces which seek to diminish attention to complexity, and to diminish integrity; by 'integrity', I mean shaping practices in accordance with principles such as truth and learning, however difficult these things might be to define. Practices which aim to standardise and measure the outcomes of teaching and research too often distort and disrupt rather than enhancing or enriching the arduous search for the best available truth which scholars and students undertake.

Richard Sennett, in an excellent set of lectures published as *The Culture of the New Capitalism*, suggests that an obsession with short-term financial gain is destroying meaningful forms of achievement associated with work in all kinds of environments.

> In the workplace [the qualities of the new economy's idealised self: the capacity to surrender, to give up possession of an established reality[21]] produce social deficits of loyalty and informal trust, they erode the value of accumulated experience. To which we should now add the hollowing out of ability.[22]

> *By probing meaning, digging deep, one risks losing time and so doing a poor job on the exam . . . purely operational thinking requires mental superficiality.*[23]

If Sennett is correct, then the threat to universities posed by short-term, instrumentalist views of the purpose education is obvious, as are the equally debilitating threats caused by leaking scarce funds to deliver reports proclaiming achievements that are largely illusory. In Sennett's view, expertise (the bedrock of the university) is being undermined by the new idea of merit that is integral to high risk, volatile capitalism. This is the moral and economic system that Prime Minister Malcolm Turnbull, a former investment banker, likes to claim presents 'all' Australians with 'opportunity'. But as Michael Pusey has noted, middle-aged manual workers laid off as part of cost-cutting in unfashionable industries do not tend to emerge a few weeks later in hubs of high-end commerce, transformed into highly-qualified risk-embracing venture capitalists.[24]

And what is missing from the world as Sennett describes it? In a simple answer I find very moving, he says, 'It is commitment'.[25] Veronica Brady modelled commitment. In her classroom, to forget the detail *or* the context was careless, while ignoring the political was not just immoral, it was bad scholarship. And here she is—*against* her time, and *ahead* of her time, on the work of intellectuals, who 'need to rediscover a dialectical sense, to play off the visible against the invisible, the actual against the possible.' Our struggle is to keep different scales of value in view, neither retreating to comfortable or distracting stories, nor becoming disabled nor hysterical about the scale of

---

21. Richard Sennett, *The Culture of the New Capitalism* (Yale University Press, 2006), 98.
22. Sennett, *The Culture of the New Capitalism*, 195.
23. Sennett, *The Culture of the New Capitalism*, 119; 120; emphasis added.
24. Michael Pusey, *Economic Rationalism in Canberra: A Nation-Building State Changes its Mind* (Melbourne: Cambridge University Press, 1991).
25. Sennett, *The Culture of the New Capitalism*, 195.

problems confronted at global and local levels—or if that is not possible, at least not to let our reading of stories end there. To conclude, let me return to *Not Wanted on the Voyage*, as Findley describes Mrs Noyes' attempts to save some of those who are 'not wanted'; they have been set on fire:

> Mrs Noyes went running—headlong down the darkening halls—her skirts and aprons yanked above her thighs— running with the blank-eyed terror of someone who cannot find her children while she hears their cries for help. Smoke was pouring through the house from one open end to the other—and at first Mrs Noyes was certain the fire must be inside, but when she reached the door and saw the blazing pyre, she knew it was not the house but something—alive— that was in flames.
>
> She paused only a second—long enough to throw up her arms against the heat and to wrap an apron around her head because the air was full sparks the size of birds and her hair was dry as tinder-grass . . .
>
> Nothing she saw that moved had feet or legs—but only arms and necks and heads—and everything was floating—heaving up through the waves of smoke, like beasts who broke the surface of a drowning-pool, then sank and broke again. And again—and then were gone.[26]

I can read this is as a story about a woman's heroism, and Mrs Noyes *is* heroic as she runs into the flames to try and effect rescues. But I think Findley wants us not just to applaud her heroism but to ask, what has created the crisis that gives Mrs Noyes such a horrifying choice between potentially suicidal heroism, and acceptance of the judgement of others about who should be cast out, burned alive? What kinds of stories, taken for granted or challenged, could lead to such a situation, could make her husband Noah think he was doing the right thing in creating mayhem and inflicting such suffering?

The questions of who is allowed 'on board', who is cast out from the polity and the consequences of that casting out, what kind of sto-

---

26. Findley, *Not Wanted on the Voyage*, 2. This passage is part of a kind of prologue, and then is repeated about a third of the way through Findley's novel.

ries are told to make sense of what is done, by whom, and how, these are questions that can be asked in the classroom, of the classroom, and of our world. These are contexts in which we often require collective action and collective reflection, we need more than the power of the individual who often finds it difficult to break free (despite the promises of Nike). Text and context, both must be attended to; so, too, individuals and society; complexity and, at the appropriate time, simplicity. By refusing to limit our focus to the individual, by insisting on scales of risk and fear appropriate to global as well as local concerns, readers and scholars of reading can help to challenge in our own time what Veronica compellingly and provocatively called '*The very grammar of perception*'.[27]

---

27. Veronica Brady, 'Intellectual Belief and Freedom', 536.

Afterword
Veronica Brady, A Personal Appreciation

Dennis Haskell

In Australia, the land of scything tall poppies, the idea of festschrifts or of other books dedicated to an individual scholar, has become increasingly difficult to sustain. This book completes a trilogy of books devoted (post mortem it seems the right word) to Veronica Brady—festschrift, biography and symposium derived study[1]—and it is a mark of her significance that they are even possible.

A festschrift is a book presented to an admired scholar on the occasion of his or her retirement, and has a long European tradition but is rare for literary or social critics in Australia—partly because publishers think there is a sorely limited market for them. When Veronica Brady was about to retire I thought she was one of those rare figures for whom it was possible—for all the reasons that are presented by the essayists in the current volume. I went to present the idea to Veronica and she was, as I thought she would be, reticently pleased but extremely hesitant about the idea. This was a privileged moment: to see Veronica hesitant was not an experience many people have had!

Fifteen years later I had the opportunity to launch Kath Jordan's biography, and I remember the occasion well. A good crowd gathered at a Perth art gallery, including the reclusive Tim Winton and other notables, and there was a great sense of occasion. Veronica Brady did speak in response but for once did not speak well; her overwhelming emotion was one of embarrassment. While we were there to celebrate her, she had no wish to celebrate herself.

---

1. *Tilting at Matilda: Literature, Aborigines, Women and the Church in Contemporary Australia*, edited by Dennis Haskell (Fremantle: Fremantle Arts Centre Press & Centre for Studies in Australian Literature, UWA, 1994); Kath Jordan, *Larrikin Angel: A Biography of Veronica Brady* (Perth: Round House P, 2009).

I mention these events because, perhaps inevitably, one of Veronica's strongest characteristics does not come out sufficiently in this book's essays: humility. She coped with the launch of the festschrift better than with the launch of the biography because its contents were essays and poems on the subjects which intensely mattered to her: literature, religion and the church, Aborigines, women and their place in Australian society. Veronica Brady sublimated her sense of self to big political and social issues, to family and friendships, and to God. This is a stance which accords perfectly with her religious belief, and it was absolutely integral to her. One reason that she inspired not just respect but a degree of devotion in others was that whatever you thought of her beliefs—and I thought she was wrong about many things—you never had any doubt about her convictions. There was nothing fake about Veronica Brady; she held her convictions fiercely because they mattered, and mattered more to her than she did to herself. She would have made a fearless martyr, and at times seemed to come close to doing so.

There were also times when she might seem to be taking you with her! A drive with Veronica at the wheel of one of the Loreto cars, especially after lunch or dinner, was a memorable experience, not one to be repeated too often! She was more at home in intellectual worlds. Gail Jones mentions her essay on White's *A Fringe of Leaves*. Before coming to Western Australia I had published an essay on the novel in which I disagreed with some aspects of her reading. Something (which I have now completely forgotten) came up over east which led me, then a much junior academic to Veronica, to go to her, a little nervously, and alert her to my article in *Southerly* and my different analysis. 'Oh, good!' she said, not in the least bothered by my temerity in disputing her interpretation of White's great novel. She wasn't bothered, in fact she seemed pleased! Many writers in this volume mention her interest in philosophers such as Paul Ricoeur. It makes perfect sense for her to be seen with hermeneutical thinkers such as Ricoeur. Hermeneutics has its roots in Biblical scholarship, and Veronica Brady's literary critical stance was one of ongoing interpretation, rather than of finished, defined views—regardless of her definiteness about various social and political positions. She was open to an ongoing process of interpretation of literary works, and indeed of linguistic works generally—more than open, she thrived on it. (Presumably Veronica did not think much of my arguments about

A Fringe of Leaves because she republished her essay in *Caught in the Draught* unchanged; I admired her for it.)

Veronica Brady, then, was always an engaging and undogmatic literary scholar. Kieran Dolin in his essay stresses the range of her reading and her resulting *bricolage*, her thinking drawn from an eclectic range of sources. To my mind she was a *bricoleur par excellence*, and could be such a bower bird because her reading and thinking was never systematic. She read like a creative writer rather than like a traditional literary critic; her conclusions were produced more by intuition than by deductive reasoning, and the range of references seem to me to have been applied more after the fact than before. This is not to say that her reading was not suggestive: it was, but just sent her along a path that she followed according to her own imagination.

Thus, her literary thinking accorded with her religious thought processes. No-one, I believe, has ever come to a belief in God through reasoning; the philosophical arguments for the existence of God come after the belief has been accepted through revelation, intuition or sheer sense of wonder. Dominic Hyde, from within the family, struggles to find grounds for her theism. Rational thought won't produce them; Veronica provides its basis in her experience of moments of 'sheer beatitude' in perceptions of nature[2]—for example, sitting in a lemon tree or gazing up at the stars. These experiences could just as well be described as moments of sheer psychological pleasure rather than of religious insight. It may well be that Veronica's background and temperament disposed her to think of them as spiritual revelations but there is no arguing against them. She told me, as she must have told others, that these epiphanies came to her at unpredictable times throughout her life.

One striking feature of this book is that the contributors come to Veronica Brady from different perspectives but are strikingly in agreement. Veronica was dedicated, imaginative, endlessly curious about the world's dimensions and their representations, determinedly progressive in her thinking and unfailingly courageous. She saw the material and spiritual as intrinsically linked, and although dedicated to Australian literature she was internationalist in outlook. Her fascination with words was inextricably tied to her fascination with the Word, in a way that is unusual amongst contemporary liter-

---

2. Recounted in Jordan, *Larrikin Angel*, 14.

ary and social scholars. As Gail Jones's essay hints, she could comfortably have lived in another age. On the other hand, one reason that she inspired students was that in some ways she remained always young—bike riding, open to new ideas, keen to explore the future. This no doubt partly derived from her belief that there was a future, even after death. Those of us who are atheists or skeptical agnostics will be very surprised if she turns out to be right; but it is a wonderful thought to imagine crossing to the other side and being greeted by a diminutive figure, glass of shiraz in hand and ready to tell us how she was debating with the angels about the denouement of *A Fringe of Leaves*, and . . . .

List of Contributors

Christine Choo is an historian, writer and social worker. Her publications include *Aboriginal Child Poverty* (1991), *Mission Girls* (2001) and a co-edited issue of *Studies in Western Australian History* entitled *History and Native Title* (2003).

Leigh Dale is a Professor in English Literature at the University of Wollongong. Leigh completed an Arts degree at UWA, doing two Australian Literature subjects and her honours thesis with Veronica Brady. She is the author of *The Enchantment of English* (2012), a history of literary studies in Australian universities, and *Responses to Self Harm* (2015).

Toby Davidson is a Senior Lecturer in English at Macquarie University, specializing in Australian poetry, with a particular focus on Christian mysticism. He is the author of *Christian Mysticism and Australian Poetry* (2013) and the editor of Francis Webb, *Collected Poems* (2011).

Kieran Dolin is an Associate Professor in English and Cultural Studies at the University of Western Australia. He is the author of *Fiction and the Law* (1999) and *A Critical Introduction to Law and Literature* (2007), and is currently working on Australian literature in the context of the *Mabo* case.

Paul Genoni is an Associate Professor in the School of Media, Culture and Creative Arts at The University of WA and is Head of the Department of Information Studies. He has published widely in Australian literary studies, including the relationship between Catholicism and Australian writing.

Dennis Haskell AM is an Emeritus Professor of English and Cultural Studies at the University of Western Australia. He is the author of several collections of poetry and many critical works, was co-editor of the literary journal *Westerly* from 1985 to 2009, and Chair of the Literature Board of the Australia Council from 2009 to 2011. He edited the festschrift for Veronica Brady, *Tilting at Matilda*, in 1994.

Tony Hughes-d'Aeth is a Senior Lecturer and chairs the discipline of English and Cultural Studies at The University of Western Australia. He is the author of *Paper Nation: The Story of the Picturesque Atlas of Australasia, 1886-1888* (Melbourne University Press, 2001) and *Like Nothing on this Earth: A Literary History of the Wheatbelt* (UWA Publishing, 2017).

Dominic Hyde is a recently-retired Senior Lecturer in Philosophy at The University of Queensland, specializing in logic and, more recently, environmental philosophy. He is the author of *Vagueness, Logic and Ontology* (2008) and *Eco-Logical Lives: the philosophical lives of Richard Routley/Sylvan and Val Routley/Plumwood* (2014).

Gail Jones is a Professor in Writing at the University of Western Sydney. She is the author of two short-story collections, a critical monograph *The Piano* (2007), and the novels *Black Mirror* (2002), *Sixty Lights* (2004), *Dreams of Speaking* (2006), *Sorry* (2007), *Five Bells* (2011) and *A Guide to Berlin* (2015).

Angeline O'Neill is discipline head of English Literature at Notre Dame Australia in Fremantle. Her teaching areas include Australian literature, Indigenous literature and Irish literature. With Anne Brewster and Rosemary van den Berg she co-edited *Those Who Remain Will Always Remember: An Anthology of Aboriginal Writing* (2000).

Terri-ann White FAHA is Director of UWA Publishing. She is a writer and editor, and has research interests in writing, fiction and publishing. Her books include a short story collection, *Night and Day* (1994), a novel, *Finding Theodore and Brina* (2001), and, as editor, *Desert Writing* and *Perth: A Guide for the Curious* (both 2016).

Curriculum Vitae:
Veronica Brady IBVM

Born, Melbourne, Australia, 5 January 1929
Died, Perth, Australia,

EDUCATIONAL HISTORY

Educated at St Francis Xavier Convent School, St Arnaud, Vic, and Loreto Convent, Toorak (Melb)
1945–50 University of Melbourne, graduating BA Honours
1965–69 University of Toronto, Canada, graduating MA and Ph D.

EMPLOYMENT HISTORY

1950   Joined the Loreto Community, the Institute of the Blessed Virgin Mary, in Ballarat, Vic.
1953–5   Senior English and History Mistress, Loreto Convent, Toorak.
1955–7   French and Geography teacher, Loreto Convent, Mary's Mount, Ballarat.
1958–61   Senior English and History Mistress, Loreto Convent, Toorak.
1961–5   Senior English and History Mistress, Loreto Convent, Kirribilli, Sydney.
1969–71   Senior Lecturer in English, Christ College Teachers College, Chadstone, Vic.
1972–5   Senior Tutor in English, University of Western Australia.
1976–9   Lecturer in English, University of Western Australia.
1980–6   Senior Lecturer in English, University of Western Australia.

1986–95   Associate Professor of English, University of Western Australia.

1996   Honorary Senior Research Fellow, Department of English, University of Western Australia.

OTHER PROFESSIONAL ACTIVITIES

1963–4   Vice-President of the English Teachers Association of New South Wales.

1964   Member of the English Curriculum Committee of the Wyndham Committee engaged in the Reform of Secondary Education in New South Wales.

1973–6   Member of the Appeals Tribunal for Western Australia of the Commonwealth Department of Social Security.

1983–6   Member of the Board of the Australian Broadcasting Commission.

1984–9   Staff-Elected Member of the Senate of the University of Western Australia.

1985–90   Member of the Board of the Library and Information Services of Western Australia.

1989   Western Australian President of PEN International.

1990–5   Member of the Board of Outcare, Western Australia.

1991–4   Chairperson for Western Australia for the Commonwealth Government Committee of Older Australians.

1993–99   Member of the Board of the Australian Theological Forum Incorporated.

2000–2   Member of the Board of the National Osteoporosis Campaign of Australia.

Research and teaching in Australian literature and culture in Universities in France, Spain, Germany, Slovenia, Austria, India, China, The Philippines, South Korea, Malaysia and Indonesia.

VISITING FELLOWSHIPS

1990   Fellowship at the Rockefeller Study Centre, Bellagio, Italy.

1994   Fellow at the Coolidge Research Colloquium, Episcopal Divinity School, Harvard University, Cambridge, USA.

2001   Rockefeller Fellowship at the University of Oregon, Eugene, Oregon, USA.

2002   Fellowship at the Rockefeller Study Centre, Bellagio, Italy.

MEMBERSHIP OF PROFESSIONAL ORGANISATIONS

The Association for the Study of Australian Literature, the European Association for Australian Studies, PEN Australia, Authors' Society of Australia, Australian and New Zealand Society for Theological Studies, Australian Theological Forum, Independent Scholars Association of Aust.

PUBLICATIONS

BOOKS

1973	*The Future People.* Melbourne Spectrum
1975	*'The Mystics'* – An introduction to the mystical tradition. Dove Publications
1979	*Crucible of Prophets.* Sydney, Theological Investigations
1992	*Caught in the Draught.* Sydney, Angus and Robertson
1997	*Can These Bones Live?* Sydney, Federation Press
1998	*South of my Days: A Biography of Judith Wright.* Sydney, Angus and Robertson

OTHER PUBLICATIONS

Over one hundred essays and articles in scholarly journals in Australia, United States of America, France, India, Italy and Spain.

CPSIA information can be obtained
at www.ICGtesting.com
Printed in the USA
FFHW020358310119
50288192-55324FF

9 781925 643756